A Right to Die?
The Dax Cowart Case

CD-ROM Teacher's Guide

Robert Cavalier and Preston K.
Covey

ROUTLEDGE

London and New York

First published 1996
by Routledge
11 New Fetter Lane, London EC4P 4EE

Simultaneously published in the USA and Canada
by Routledge
29 West 35th Street, New York, NY 10001

Routledge is an International Thomson Publishing company

© 1996 Routledge

Designed and typeset in Palatino by Gooch
Printed and bound in Great Britain by Clays Ltd, St Ives PLC

ISBN   0–415–15274–7
ISBN   0–415–91754–9 (multiple user pack)

Contents

Preface

In the so-called "Golden Age," in the beginnings of the Western philosophical tradition in Greece before its ascent into Platonic abstraction, one vehicle for theory was the theater. Universal elements of "the human condition" were reflected by chorus and convention in the concrete, compelling drama of Greek tragedy and comedy.

A Right to Die? was the first in a series of interactive multimedia programs developed under Project THEORIA, whose agenda is reflected in its acronym: Testing Hypotheses in Ethics: Observation, Reason, Imagination, and Affect. The goal of Project THEORIA is to design compelling, interactive multimedia environments – sensoriums – for exploring hypotheses in the domain of human values.

Theoria (Greek for *theory*) is also an allusion to the concept of theory rooted in concrete observation and draws upon the common etymological root of both *theory* and *theater* in the ancient Greek verb *theorein:* to see, to view, to behold. Project THEORIA seeks to provide a theater for ethical theory – to bring it to ground in observable, palpable, affecting contexts that are rich in the experiential complexity that any competent theory must first behold in order to explain. Skills of moral reasoning, like the practical skills of the surgeon or the theoretical skills of the scientist, require an operating theater or laboratory for practice. Our aim is to exploit interactive technology to provide a good analog of that theater or laboratory for the study of ethics.

Development of *A Right to Die?* in analog videodisc format (Falcon Software, 1990) was funded in part by grants from the

Alfred P. Sloan Foundation, the Claude Worthington Benedum Foundation, the Andrew W. Mellon Foundation, and the Pew Memorial Trusts. It received the EDUCOM Best Humanities Software Award in 1989. The current version has been substantially revised in digital CD (compact disc) format.

We thank Scott Roberts, who designed the prototype videodisc version; David Andersen and Steven Bend, who provided invaluable programming support for the subsequent videodisc versions; Dr. Joe Henderson, for Dartmouth College's design and development of the Macintosh Hypercard™-based version of the videodisc; Liz Style and John Zimmerman, who digitized the video for the CD version; and Kate Maloy, who provided the original narrative version of Dax's case for this manual.

We also thank Dr. Robert B. White; Marie B. Gale, Professor of Psychiatry at the University of Texas Medical Branch, Galveston, TX, for granting the rights to use the film documentary *Please Let Me Die*; Choice in Dying in New York City for the rights to use the film documentary *Dax's Case*; and Dr. Stuart Youngner of the Case Western Reserve University School of Medicine for his consultation and guidance in the beginning when this project was but an abstract concept.

We wish especially to acknowledge Dax Cowart, whose story is the heart of this CD, as our primary inspiration. This project is dedicated to the courage of Dax Cowart and people like him who exemplify moral life and inquiry in their most challenging forms.

System Requirements

This CD-ROM can be installed and used on either an IBM-compatible PC running Microsoft Windows™ or on an Apple Macintosh™.

All details below are minimum requirements.*

Windows Version

80386 processor or higher
MS-DOS™ 3.3 or higher
Microsoft Windows™ 3.1 or higher
SVGA graphics card and monitor
8 MB of RAM
2 MB available hard disk space
ISO 9660 compatible CD-ROM drive
MSCDEX 2.2 or higher
Mouse, audio board, Video for Windows

Macintosh Version

68020 processor or higher
System 6.0.8 or higher
Macintosh CD-ROM and Quicktime™ extensions
2 MB memory (800K free RAM)
1 MB free hard disk space
ISO 9660 compatible CD-ROM drive

*For best results, a 4x CD-ROM drive is recommended. For best screen display on a Macintosh, set the monitor to "thousands of colors".

Windows Installation Instructions

Start your Windows application.
From **File Manager**, select **Run**.
Type "D:\setup" and press <return> (where "D" is the letter representing your CD-ROM drive).
Follow on-screen instructions.

Start-up Instructions

Windows

Start your Windows application.
Double-click on the **Dax** icon in the Dax Program Group.

Macintosh

Open the CD-ROM icon by double-clicking on it with your mouse.
Double-click on the **Dax** icon.

Introduction

The Case

Some years ago, Donald (Dax) Cowart, an unmarried 25-year-old man, returned from active duty in the Air Force and, while waiting for a job in the airlines industry, worked in real estate development. One summer's day, Dax drove out to look at some unpopulated land that he was considering as an investment. As he was getting ready to leave, his attempt to start his car set off an explosion in a buried but leaking gas pipeline. Dax received second- and third-degree burns over two-thirds of his body. At the time that we encouter Dax in treatment, his injuries have left

Donald (Dax) Cowart

him severely scarred, his hands are badly deformed, and the sight in his one remaining eye is at risk. As a patient, he undergoes daily treatments in an antiseptic tank – tankings that are so painful to him that he has persistently asked the doctors to stop his treatment. Dax feels that the length of his projected treatment and the quality of life that he can expect to regain do not warrant the torment he must suffer. The doctors know that if they continue his treatment, he will live; if they stop his treatment, he will surely die. A basic question posed at this point of impasse between Dax and his care givers is: Does Dax have a right to die? If so, what does this mean?

The CD-ROM provides an interactive multimedia environment in which to explore this and related issues in the case of Dax Cowart.

This *Teacher's Guide* incorporates features of the *User Guide* that accompanies single-user copies of the program: **System Requirements**, an **Overview of the Program for Users**, and an expanded section on **Further Annotated Resources**. The system information and program overview may be copied and placed with distributed CDs. In addition, this guide contains the following sections:

A Rationale for this Interactive Multimedia Case Study

This essay discusses the motivation behind the development of the CD-ROM and our designs for its use. Because the essay refers to personal experiences of one of the authors, Preston Covey, a first-person address is sometimes employed. A natural question about educational media concerns what advantage one medium offers over another. For example, what is the "value added" of an interactive multimedia case study over a linear video or a well-wrought narrative presentation? While he assumes complementarity among these media, Covey attempts to delineate the special advantages of the interactive format. He also reflects on the role of concrete, emotion-laden case studies in ethics education and the issue of evaluating the efficacies of different educational media for their presentation.

A Sample Pedagogical Tour for Teachers

This section provides quick familiarity with the basic features and contents of the program, with some comments on pedagogy for teachers.

Strategies for Use

This section discusses various ways in which the CD can be employed in a course setting, as well as logistical and practical deployment issues.

A Narrative Version of Dax's Case

This narrative was constructed to be (roughly) "informationally equivalent" to the video content and structure of the CD's **Guided Inquiries**. Instructors may provide students with copies of the narrative for review or as a memory aid after they have explored the CD presentation. The narrative may also be used to explore with students the differential impact of a compelling narrative of Dax's case as compared with linear or interactive video presentations.

Select Bibliography

This lists the resources referred to in the other parts of this manual.

A Rationale for this Interactive Multimedia Case Study

An ancient pagoda proverb reminds us rudely of what we know too well:

A ship of theory, when launched upon the sea of facts, often sinks.

Summary

Pace conventional wisdom that warns against emotional appeal and fallacies, the emotions and particularities of raw moral experience provide essential data for both ethical judgment and ethical theory. The difficult balancing act, the assay of our emotions and reasons together, can be learned only through practice: one function of education or training. Interactive multimedia provides a theater for importing experiential reality into the classroom, a safe exploratorium to enable practice in balancing emotional engagement and critical reflection. Interactive multimedia provides a hybrid environment that complements more traditional media, such as books and film, to address a major challenge in ethics education: finding ways to accommodate, integrate, and balance both emotion and reason, both powerful experience and careful analysis – a challenge not unknown to science itself. One advantage of interactive multimedia is its combination of two features of experiential learning – a fundament of all learning:

1 compelling visual experience to engage the emotions and extend the moral imagination where first-hand experience is lacking – like film, but unlike books;

2 computer interaction to challenge the viewer, to afford the

viewer control as well as access to research resources, to enable reflection – like books, but unlike film.

In this essay, Preston Covey argues that emotional and, *ipso facto*, experiential engagement is essential to the study of ethics and that interactive multimedia can serve two essential and complementary modes of ethical inquiry and education: engagement and detachment. He assumes a first-person address in recalling some key experiences as a teacher, which motivated his own turn to interactive multimedia for ethics education. This essay is adapted and expanded from earlier versions: "Ethics and the Crucible of Experience: *A Right to Die?*," in Jerome Johnston and Robert B. Kozma (eds), *The Computer in Humanities Education* (New Haven, CT: Yale University Press, 1995); "The Crucible of Experience," in Robert Heeger and Theo van Willigenberg (eds), *The Turn to Applied Ethics* (Kampen, Netherlands: Kok Pharos Publishing House, 1993).

Design and Ethics: The Adjustment of Means to Ends under Constraints

When the mapping of actions on states of the world is problematic, then, and only then, are we faced with genuine problems of design.
(Simon, 1977)

Design, like ethics, entails, as Herbert Simon put it well, *the adjustment of means to ends under constraints*. The ends may be various: artifacts, functionalities, performances, states of affairs, states of mind. The means may be various resources, instrumentalities, actions, artifacts. The constraints may be various limitations in resources, in functionality, or in possibility: physical, temporal, moral, monetary, political, psychological, technological. Many factors can make the adjustment of means to ends problematic. The severity of the operative constraints is only one of them. Trade-offs among alternative means is another. But design problems begin and end with ends: ends dictate problem definition, the selection of means, specifications for implementation, success criteria, and standards of evaluation. All design presupposes some desired ends, goals, objectives, purposes, or effects. One can neither design, nor fashion, nor evaluate a tool, for example, without a notion of what it is supposed to be good for or what problem it is supposed to solve. So, other important factors that can make a design task seriously problematic are conflicting ends, unclear priorities among ends, ill-defined ends, or contestable ends. Classic cases are attempts to design solutions to complex problems (such as toxic waste disposal, the national debt, world peace, or how best to educate people in ethics).

The design of solutions to educational problems is seriously problematic in several ways. For one thing, it takes place on many levels: from defining the specific problem(s) to be solved, to selecting the content, activities, tools, or strategies (means) that promise to promote the desired effects (ends), to implementing an appropriate program of instruction, learning or action (adjusting means to ends), to evaluating (judging or measuring) whether the desired effects are (or are likely to be) realized (whether the means can achieve – or are well adapted to promote – the ends). If one is designing an interactive computer-based multimedia environment, the selection process entails choosing among both development and deployment platforms, programming or authoring tools, and multimedia resources. Implementation entails designing a program of interactive instruction or learning, an interface for displaying and accessing the multimedia resources, and control software. Evaluation involves designing or adapting evaluation instruments sensitive to the desired effects. The design task, in any case, begins and ends with ends: instructional or learning goals, and their desired effects. And these are notoriously debatable, often hard to define, and unhappily hard to assess.

If design entails *the adaptation of means to ends under constraints*, the logically prior and crucial problem for design is the clarification of ends and priorities (the adjustment of ends amongst themselves), which, at bottom, answer to arguable human values. In the design of educational media, the very educational problems we choose to address are ultimately dictated by arguable human values and protean human priorities – personal, professional, social, political, and so on. It is no accident that when we speak of people's "designs," we often mean their intentions or objectives. In ethics, presuppositions about ends and means must be made explicit. Therefore, this essay emphasizes the rationale for resorting to multimedia technology in the first place, rather than the technical details of implementation. In keeping with the spirit of illustration (by meager anecdote) as opposed to abstraction (within the full-blown frame of formal theory), I will focus on certain problems in ethics education that motivated my own resort to interactive multimedia (as a case in point), the features of the technology that proffer solutions to these problems, and the reasons that those problems are important and the solutions hard to assess.

Teaching Ethics: Observations from the Trenches

Ethics and the teaching of ethics may be a mysterious or at least unfamiliar business to many observers outside the field. But we, *qua* human beings, are all engaged in the raw material for study in ethics: moral experience. That raw material is inescapable in life, but often ignored, at a cost, in the classroom. Ethics education has two crucial and complementary modes: detachment and engagement. Each admits of kinds and degrees. Metaphorically speaking, if detachment is a function of the head (or intellect), engagement is a function of head, heart, and viscera – all three. At the extremes, engagement typifies raw moral experience at first hand, while detachment typifies the theoretical turn in academic ethics, which examines moral problems and experience at some tractable distance. Albert Jonsen (1991) offers other useful metaphors for contrasting modes of detachment and engagement: the balloon riding high above the terrain of moral life and the bicycle riding its maze of rough and winding roads at close quarters. I am concerned here with the experience of the bicyclist, with the need to educate our students with sweaty bicycle tours as well as with lofty balloon rides and cartography; the need to induce moral experience, engagement with moral realities, within the ivory tower. To illustrate, I begin with some anecdotes from my own experience in the teaching trenches.

Anecdote #1

Students, young students especially, may have little sense of the predicaments of other people, and they may often take leave of their own sensibilities and fail to appreciate their own predicaments. I remember well the day that a student had the temerity in class discussion to object (the case at issue is irrelevant): *But that would be lying!* A wave of guffaws rolled out of the back row of football players, a male chorus announcing to the class their macho worldly-wise cynicism, *Like, hey, so what?* What was going on here? A typical lapse. People take leave of their senses, especially in classrooms. In this case, the football players took leave of their sense of the stake they have in whether people, as a rule, lie or don't lie. I don't know whether this is a special problem in the philosophy classroom – that students lose touch with what they really care about – but I looked for ways to counter this phenomenon of detached sensibility.

For one thing, I began using films in class, an obvious stratagem for importing a little reality. There was the case of the Downs Syndrome baby with duodenal atresia (blockage of the esophagus). The question was: May the parents deny permission for surgery to correct the blockage, thereby causing their mongoloid infant to die of starvation? The film showed the agony of the parents' decision to withhold surgery, the agony of the infant's slow death by starvation. Film over, lights on, dead silence, no motion to leave. Of course, who could fail to be moved? So what? In the next class, two days later, I asked the students for their reactions to the film. Most expressed surprise as well as dismay. Surprise at something they had not thought about in reading about the case before viewing the film. Surprise to see how painful it was for the nurses who had to watch that infant die under their care, for two whole weeks. But, I pointed out, we read and talked about the objections of the medical staff to the decision. *Yes,* one student exclaimed, *but we didn't realize what that would be like . . . what it would be like for the nurses.*

This is an example of emotional engagement with a moral reality: in this case, the perception of the palpable interests of others who are suffering pain and moral perplexity. The crucial effect here was not just the inchoate emotional impact of the film on the students. Rather, it was their specific surprise, their *discovery* of something specific that they had failed to imagine previously: the palpability of the nurses' suffering, the compelling interest the nursing staff had in not suffering that infant's death. *What difference does it make to be aware of the nurses' feelings if they don't decisively tip the scales in the case?*, I asked. That, we all agreed, was an intriguing question. One lesson, perhaps, was that some things have to be seen to be felt or even imagined, particularly respecting the interests of others.

Anecdote #2

Films were one obvious pedagogical resource, a tactic for putting students in touch with common human interests, sensibilities, or predicaments. Thought-experiments, sometimes in the guise of lies, were another. In another class, the topic was the typical: *Who gets the kidney dialysis machine? How should we decide?* The papers I received rehearsed the standard arguments from the readings, pro and con. I told the class that their papers were lackluster, facile in their treatment of the cases, unimaginative about what they considered to be relevant or what further information they needed to make a decision; *Time* magazine could do better. In summary, I said, I didn't think they gave a damn about who got the kidney treatment or how. *How is that supposed to make a philosophy paper better?*, someone asked. A good question. I needed an *experimentum crucis.*

So I lied. I told the class that I had gotten the cases from a colleague on the ethics committee at Presbyterian Hospital; that these were real patients, alive today, awaiting a decision on treatment, some of whom, without that treatment, would surely die within weeks or months. I said that these patients had agreed to read the students' papers, and that I was going to give them these papers to read, with the students names blanked out, for their reaction or edification. The students were stunned; some were angry.

You can't do that!, someone objected.

Why not? Why do you care?, I asked. *They won't know who you are.*

No quick answer to this.

Why do you care?, I asked again.

We didn't think they were real, someone said.

What difference does it make?, I pressed. *Your papers aren't going to decide the case. Wouldn't it be interesting to know what they think? Aren't you curious?*, I teased.

That's gross!, someone said.

So you care about these people's feelings?

Of course.

What about who gets the life-saving treatment?

Of course.

If I were to give your papers to the patients or ethics committee, would you want a chance to rewrite them?

Of course.

Why? Do you think anything you might say now will make any difference?

Probably not.

Then why rewrite them? What difference could it make?

That's not the point.

Yes? Well, what is *the point?*

We all agreed that was an intriguing question; and that they would rewrite their papers. One student asked: *Would you really have done that? Are those really real people?* I said that I wouldn't and they weren't, but asked again if they would still like to rewrite their papers anyway.

Yes. Unanimous.

What a reality trip!, someone said.

And no one questioned why I had lied.

Anecdote #3

Getting personal, say, by "ad hominem" or appeal to emotion, was another tactic for putting students in touch with their sensibilities and predicaments. "Ad hominem" and "appeal to emotion" are classic categories of fallacy. This is curious, since most "fallacies," much of the time, are indispensable to all manner of inquiry: Where would law courts be without the "ad hominem"? "Appeals to emotion" (the so-called "pathetic fallacy," derived from the Greek *pathos*, for feeling, especially suffering) are an especially pathetic case of "fallacy" because susceptibility to emotional appeal is one of the most precious human capacities in moral life. Appeals to emotion, sensibility, and feeling are essential to doing ethics; emotions, like moral "intuitions," are admissible evidence. We must understand, of course, that they are not dispositive: fallacy derives from jumping to conclusions solely on the basis of emotion. But appeals to emotion are no less crucial in pedagogy. Case in point – the following case might be called "The Sophist Sandbags the Sophomore":

A distinguished philosopher of science (I'll call him "Professor") was our guest speaker at the Philosophy Club one evening. The topic was "Dilemmas of Free Will and Determinism." Professor was having a devil of a time getting one sophomore student (I'll call him "Determined") to admit any intuitive appeal whatever for the notion of free will. Determined thought this notion was one of the great gratuitous delusions of the opiated masses. Determined was genuinely, if ironically, indignant that anyone would be weak willed enough to believe in "free will." Kindly and patient, Professor tried every angle he could think of to get Determined to *see* the appeal of the idea, to *sense* and admit that important consequences followed from its denial – else we have no dilemma! Determined could only smile indulgently; that was precisely his position: there is no dilemma here, there is simply no substance to this fuzzy illusory commodity, and rational kind will give it up! Throughout this discussion, Determined's girlfriend was all aglow over his performance and demonstrably affectionate. Determined fairly gloated over her attentions. At one point, the girl gently kissed Determined on his cheek. Determined smiled at her, the very picture of happy young love. At this point I joined the dialogue, which I paraphrase as follows:

Determined, uh, sorry, but I couldn't – I'm sure we all couldn't – help noticing: your girl friend is very fond of you, and you of her; she just kissed you. That was nice. You liked that? *Sure.* You think she meant it, to be nice, to show you she likes you, loves you? *Sure.* Do you think she loves you, that that's why she kissed you? *Sure.* And you really think she meant it? *Yeah, sure; what do you mean?* You really think her kissing you meant something? You feel it meant something that she felt like kissing you, that she likes to kiss you, that she did kiss you – rather than, say, not kissing you or, say, . . . sneezing, or biting her fingernail? You think this kiss was something she did sincerely, not just something that, say, just happened, like a sneeze or a hiccup or a twitch? *Sure, yeah, sure; what's the deal?* Well, I was just wondering why you, since you are such a hardball determinist, why you feel this thing she did has any more meaning than, say, a leaf falling off a tree . . . a heart beating its beat . . . or her chewing her gum or fidgeting with her ring . . . or her not doing these things or . . . anything else? Can you tell me why you attach special meaning to her kiss, when, in your hardball determinist view, it's just like a billiard ball bouncing off another ball bouncing off another ball in the great chain of deterministic hardball? How do you reconcile the meaning you give to her kiss with your determinism? Perhaps you give it special meaning because you're determined to do so? Or, perhaps, you feel a little tug, a little compulsion to believe that she did this nice thing out of her own, dare I say it, . . . free will?

That was a terrifying moment for me, because I didn't know whether he, or she, would feel hurt. But the ploy worked. That does not mean that Determined became a believer in free will, whatever that might mean; I have no idea about that, nor was that my point. To conclude that determinism was false from my *experimentum crucis* would indeed have been fallacious and fatuous. I provided no refutation of determinism, any more than Dr. Johnson refuted skepticism by kicking a stone. I merely induced an experience, at a risk (well aware that we take ethical risks in the name of pedagogy, never mind education). The student suddenly found himself not refuted, but engaged, indeed possessed – possessed by the common human sensation of the ineluctable allure of the idea of "free will," the common human sense that vague but important things did seem to hang on this warm, fuzzy and strong sensation; things that he deeply cared about, that he could neither exactly explain nor explain away. He was possessed, perhaps, by the palpable sensation of dilemma. Having monopolized the discussion to this point, he could now only say that he honestly didn't know what to say. In wonder, we are told (and, perhaps, in its silence), begins philosophy. I believe that this student was simply beginning to experience wonder. He was just beginning to take the dilemmas of free will and determinism seriously, to discover "the importance of what we care about" (Frankfurt, 1988) and the felt predicaments that underlie conceptual conundrums, with some emotional edge.

Anecdote #4

Many years ago, in a *Wall Street Journal* op-ed piece entitled "When Values Are Substituted for Truth," William J. Bennett related a similarly ironic conversation from an ethics class: a conversation about another sophomoric preoccupation, ethical relativism. (William Bennett, who is perhaps known for having served as Secretary of Education in the U.S., is a philosophy Ph.D. and was once a philosophy teacher. I believe, however, that he may have borrowed this tale or the stratagem – or that, in any case, his pedagogical ploy is originally attributable to the famously clever Sidney Morgenbesser of Columbia University.) I have adapted and used this stratagem many times myself over the years. I paraphrase the scenario:

> *Student:* I don't think that you can teach ethics because there really aren't any in any real sense. Each person's values are as good as anyone else's. Values are subjective.
>
> *Teacher:* No, on the contrary, I say that's not true. Some people's values are better than others'.
>
> *Student:* No, they're subjective. No one can impose his values on somebody else.
>
> *Teacher:* Well, then, what do you think of this? I say values are not subjective and, if you don't agree with me, then I'll flunk you.
>
> *Student:* You can't do that! Are you crazy?
>
> *Teacher:* No. I'm surely not crazy. And I can do that. *Why not?*

Student: Well . . . uh . . . because . . . because it's . . . it's not *fair* !

This is another case of bringing home the consequences of one's position with real emotional impact. It is certainly an appeal, of sorts, to emotion.

Now, emotions can compel people to jump to premature, ill-considered, or biased conclusions, but emotional quandaries can also confound facile judgment, countermand prejudice, and induce an appreciation of the complexity of a problem. In some cases, emotion can compel a realistic perception of moral problems.

> Perhaps the most frustrating feature of describing a moral problem is the gulf between moral description and moral experience. No description, it seems, can do justice to the realities of our moral problems. It is extraordinarily difficult, if not impossible, to capture the countless subtleties that go into the perceptions and judgments of each person involved . . . the conflicting emotions.
>
> (Elliott, 1992)

Too often students (and teachers) approach the consideration of moral problems as abstract, academic exercises, devoid of the excruciating perplexities of real life moral choices and their problematic commitments. This is often so because they have none but abstract, denatured descriptions of the situations at issue and are removed by some comforting or convenient distance from the direct experience of problematicity.

Consider the case of Dax Cowart: Dax was a young man involved in a tragic accident that, in the end, took his sight and left him burned and grossly scarred over two-thirds of his body, with little use of his hands. As part of his burn therapy, he was subjected for fourteen months to daily, multiple, excruciatingly painful antiseptic tankings, cleansing and debridement of his wounds. Dax continually and lucidly asked – indeed, demanded – to have the treatments discontinued. This would certainly have resulted in massive infection and death; a fact that he knew. Does Dax have a right to refuse treatments that would certainly save his life, although they would leave him, against his will, as a (quote) "blind cripple"? Would his right to die entail a right against any of his care givers, who then would be obligated to help him to die? And how would the hospital, in both concrete procedures and general policy terms, "accommodate" Dax in his wish to terminate treatment?

I have just given a relatively abstract, or brief, but typical case statement. What do we need to know, consider, and weigh in order to decide such issues? With such an abstract description, we can merely speculate – or wonder what has been left out. How much more description or information is needed to allow us to make a responsible judgment in such a case? How would we wish others to decide our own case, were we in Dax's predicament? How would *we* decide Dax's predicament, were it left to us to decide? What more would we want or need to know? Why? What difference would it make? These are crucial issues in the matter of both ethical judgment in the instant case, and in the construction of sound ethical theory in the general case.

As it happens, there is a documentary film about Dax's case that vivifies the sort of subtle, qualitative, and affective information – the so-called "facts of the case" – that is difficult to describe or convey by non-visual media. The bare narrative "facts" of Dax's case tell us that Dax's hands are nearly useless, that his treatment is extremely painful, that his mother and doctors refuse to release Dax from treatment, contrary to his own articulate demands. The qualitative *realities* behind these bare *facts* are vividly evident in the documentary film. Visualization conveys a direct experiential sense of crucial questions: *How useless* are Dax's hands? *How painful* is his treatment? *How uncertain* does the future quality of his life *seem* to him? *What difference* does this make? How do his mother and doctors *feel* about letting Dax die without treatment? *What difference* does this make? *How lucid* is Dax? And, as you *see* it, would *you* be willing to undergo Dax's treatment and lead his life in similar straits? As you *see* it, would *you* be willing to take active measures to let or help Dax die? Again, some problems must be seen to be imagined, to be analyzed responsibly, to be resolved sensitively. Visual material conveys the sort of raw, experiential data required by our moral sensorium for responsible analysis of ethical issues; that is, analysis that is not only *principled* or *theoretically grounded* but also *responsive* to the emotional and practical burdens of all parties to the case. Some "facts" are better experienced than described.

For six years, I presented Dax's case using traditional narrative case study materials. The typical result was that students had difficulty "seeing" and aptly representing the ethical problems and conflicting viewpoints in the case. No surprise – how can we expect students to construct an apt and compelling representation of an ethical problem or viewpoint from a denatured case abstract? The needed but often neglected resource in ethics education is palpable, concretely situated experience. As Robert Fullinwider (1988) has observed:

> If moral learning is essentially learning by doing, then *the central and ongoing resource for moral education is experience, real or vicarious* . . . [In school] limitations of time, place, resources and structure mean that any major broadening of moral experience must come by way of *vicariously* living through the moral lives of others . . . in literature . . . history . . . through stories.
>
> [emphasis added]

Lack of attention to the experiential component of ethics, including its attendant emotions and engaged sensibilities, is compounded by our conventional ambivalence about the role of emotion in ethical reasoning. A popular, if useful, myth perpetuated by conventional textbook wisdom is that we must always deliberate impartially and unemotionally. In actual fact, *we do not* and *we can not*, in any strict sense. This is at best a good rule of thumb. Impartiality is a formal, regulative ideal. In our fallibility, in material reality, we weigh a plurality of competing interests, as best we can. The question is how we do so, or best learn to do so, appropriately. In this task, emotions are, literally, *informative* (cf. Gordon, 1987).

Our sensibilities inform our moral perceptions and are informed in turn by details of experience beyond anything that we can adequately describe. For example, anger can be prima facie evidence of wrongdoing. Fear may carry an accurate perception of risk or threat. Emotional hurt, like physical pain, may accurately signal important harm. Our emotions alert us to the very commodities we seek to protect by any system of moral rules: our interests, our values, "the importance of what we care about" (Frankfurt, 1988). Emotions are indicators of threatened welfare. Emotions bear testimony. Emotions are raw data for inquiry. Emotions are, at the bar of ethics, admissible evidence. The challenge is to know what exactly to make of them, as an evidentiary or probative matter.

One mark of competent ethical judgment, by any textbook account, is the consideration of the consequences of our actions. The consequences of a decision, action, policy, or general rule (moral, legal, or whatever) cannot be assessed without a vivid representation of the interests of others who will be affected by it. The trick is not simply to learn to put ourselves in the other person's "shoes" or circumstance, but to learn to put ourselves in another's "skin," perspective, or feelings. Knowing what I would do in your situation does not necessarily let me understand what you happen to feel in your situation or what you happen to care about. In other words, ethics demands both more intellectual work and more emotional work on our part than the "Golden Rule." To represent an ethical issue, to perceive that there exists an ethical problem, requires an appreciation of the threatened values and interests of the other affected stakeholders. This task is essential to our theoretical speculations – for example, about the deliverances of a utilitarian calculus or the hypothetical "social contract" (Solomon, 1990) – as well as to our most prosaic practical deliberations. Identifying and vividly representing the interests of others is essential both to weighing the consequences of our actions and to debating the terms of any social contract or system of rules by which we expect to be bound. In sum, either perceiving a moral problem, or making an ethical judgment, or theorizing about ethics is, at bottom, and ineluctably, a matter of the *imaginative identification with the details of others' lives* (Rorty, 1989). The raw material is provided by emotion-laden experience and, no less than in science, by close observation of the human circumstances in which such emotion arises.

Ends: What Are Our Goals in Ethics Education?

Non scholae, sed vitae dicimus.
[Not for school, but for life do we learn – Epistolae Morales]

Students may have difficulty appreciating many ethical issues in classroom settings. It is difficult to teach about dilemmas in which complex ethical considerations vie for attention and resolution. Moral reflection and imagination require an experiential crucible, an analog to the scientist's laboratory or field work, rich in the palpable complexity of "real life" that is impossible to ignore, where choices must be made under duress and uncertainty and consequences suffered. The feeling that some problems are not real until they beset us (a costly form of education) can be obviated by sharper perception of the problems of others. Vicariously sharing others' defeat in the face of problems incapable of clear or felicitous solution – problems of surprising dimensions – undercuts the often facile, judgmental reactions that controversial questions raise in both the political arena and the classroom. But it is understandably hard for students to perceive or appreciate problems that they have not experienced at first hand.

The study of ethics is too often academic and speculative in the worst senses of those terms. In serious science education we expect students to handle apparatus and process data that is rich in both quantity and quality. In ethics we more typically rely on intellectual apparatus alone and demand neither quantity nor quality in the data to be explained. Nor are we accustomed to introducing raw data into our studies, being more comfortable with the abstract, tractable commodities of detached academic discourse: well-formed propositions, arguments, reasons, concepts, and denatured case studies. But these are not enough if our aim is education for life in the wider world rather than careers in the rarefied or insulated groves of academe.

Consider the analogy: We do not attempt to teach science by acquainting students with scientific method through books and hot-air disputations alone (even in most high schools). We do not teach scientific theory abstracted from some hands-on experience with how it is constructed, by both individual effort and social collaboration. Science education involves not only the theoretical content of science, but also its art, its craft, its texture, its headaches, its social context, its venality and frustrations at first hand. Put another way, we would not think of credentialing scientists, engineers, surgeons, or other artists without providing them some hands-on experience with the actual stuff and rude realities of "real life" practice.

Consider the contrast: Ethics is typically taught by exposing students, through books and hot-air disputations, to verbiage. The verbiage is presumably artful, rigorous, insightful, and about matters of great concern and practical import. But it is typically occupied with the analysis of abstract ideas and arguments about these matters. By contrast, in life, ethical problems come trammeled with confounding immediacy, detail, and emotion, whereas the classroom is experientially barren, devoid of the stuff of moral experience, with meager data in minute quantity, problems faintly glimpsed at a safe theoretical distance, and propositions analyzed to a practically impotent fare-thee-well. Academic ethics is typically preoccupied with its own abstract conceits and grossly underwhelmed by the data and realities of moral experience from across the daunting spectrum of human life. This is conspicuously the case in how slightly ethical theory takes account of human emotion and sensibility, problematic forces – and invaluable resources – in moral affairs. Apart from a few classical thinkers (for example, Aristotle and Hume) and a growing contemporary literature creditable, in large part, to female academics (for example, Baier, 1985; Callahan, 1988; Kittay and Meyers, 1987; Midgley, 1981; Noddings, 1984; Nussbaum, 1996; Rosenberg, 1986; Solomon, 1990; Tavris, with Paul, 1990), emotions and feelings have been disparaged as sources of mere fallacy and bias, forces to be neutralized or overcome in ethical reasoning.

The limitations of rational decision models are not even as fully acknowledged in ethical theory as they are in economic or political ones. It is ironic that a salient book on the role of emotion in the province of reason, *Passion Within Reason: The Strategic Role of the Emotions*, was written by an economist (Frank, 1988); yet another frankly considers the practical importance of empathic capacities for crisis management in business (Pauchant and Mitroff, 1992). Is ethics so impractical that it cannot learn from economics or business? The epistemic and evidence-bearing functions of emotion in ethical reasoning require more critical study than they have received in philosophy (cf. Gordon, 1987). Teachers of ethics need to become more involved with the empirical dimensions of ethical reasoning: for example, observing how people in fact wrestle with ethical issues under emotional duress (see, for example,

Kurtines and Gewirtz, 1984, 1987; Petraglia, 1991; Schoeman, 1987).

In sum, too many real-world problems for which we aim to equip our students are not well captured in books, lectures, or class discussion. These media cannot always *simulate* the practical realities or *stimulate* the human sensibilities that motivate and confound moral problems. Typical students lack one important commodity for the study of ethics: life experience – or enough of it, in all the right places (else we would be divine, not human). Typical academic settings lack adequate means to provide access to the rich, affecting data of "real life" dilemmas that reveal our own conflicted values and allow us to identify with those of others. In *Teaching Values in College*, Richard Morrill (1981) provides a commonsensical framework for values education, consisting of three dimensions:

1 values analysis, the explicit articulation of the values, principles, and concepts that underlie our value judgments and choices (a priority focus of traditional ethics courses);

2 values consciousness, where two crucial components are self-knowledge (discovering and "owning" one's own often inchoate, competing values) and empathy (coming to identify with or understand the values of others); and

3 values criticism, which raises questions about the values posited or discovered (another priority of traditional or philosophic ethics courses).

Values consciousness (both self- and other-regarding) is a difficult objective to define or implement in academic settings, but it is crucial and material to the analytic and critical tasks of philosophic ethics. It is remarkable how little articulate students can demonstrate of their very own values, never mind the values of others.

Means: Interactive Multimedia Possibilities

Multimedia here refers to any interactive computer-based environment that dynamically links several media: text, graphics, animation, sound, and full-color, high-quality video (motion or still). Interactivity between the user and the program (with varying degrees of user control) and dynamic connectivity among the several media are features that distinguish computer-based multimedia environments from passive linear audio-visual media like television or film. Interactive video and laser-optical media are other terms for essentially the same concept, but multimedia has been widely adopted as a generic term.

> With all its powers, the computer cannot contribute much to the learning of open-ended subjects like moral philosophy . . . fields of knowledge that cannot be reduced to formal rules and procedures.
>
> (Bok, 1985)

Derek Bok's allegation is certainly true in its second claim. And the second claim may seem good reason for believing the first, if one's model is the computer as expert system or automated tutor: the computer as teacher. But if one takes seriously the role of the computer as navigational aid for an experiential learning environment (as persuasively described by Bok in the same paper), then the first claim hardly follows. In this role, computer-based multimedia can provide new channels to moral experience, added stimuli to moral imagination, as well as new opportunities for reflection on that experience. Multimedia environments are useful for the rich data, texture, and context they allow us to import into experientially barren groves of academic study – allied with interactive computer technology for the easy control, flexible exploration, and disciplined reflection it can induce.

> Five decades of research suggest that there are no learning benefits to be gained from employing different media in instruction, regardless of their obviously attractive features or advertised superiority . . . media are mere vehicles that deliver instruction but do not influence student achievement any more than a truck that delivers our groceries causes changes in nutrition.
>
> (Clark, 1983)

The term *media* is ambiguous. If we exploit this ambiguity, Richard Clark's notorious truck metaphor is useful for gainsaying or at least limiting the generalization it conveys, which (to be fair) applies to formal instruction in the content and methods of science and mathematics. We need to ask: What if certain groceries are not delivered at all? Nutrition might surely suffer. One modest aim of multimedia for ethics is simply to deliver raw material and reflective opportunities not deliverable by non-visual, non-interactive media. For delivering vivid experience as well as reflective control, for exploiting the combined power of visualization and interactivity, interactive multimedia is a vehicle without obvious alternatives, like a "wet lab" in chemistry or biology.

But interactive multimedia environments can also serve as vehicles for illustrating techniques, for practicing skills, and for delivering the research resources of a library – conveniently accessible at the user's fingertips within one continuous environment. At the Center for the Advancement of Applied Ethics (CAAE) at Carnegie Mellon University, we have undertaken several interactive multimedia projects to explore the potential of this technology. Our mission, in terms of what ethics education demands and how technology can help, is better illustrated by a variety of projects than by one salient example alone, but I will describe here our foremost project, *A Right to Die? The Dax Cowart Case.* Each of our projects seeks to pose questions about which there is general controversy; to present engaging case studies, "rabbit holes," as it were, leading into a complex underground warren of issues, which begin an experiential odyssey in which explorers, like Alice in Wonderland, must struggle to maintain their own bearings; and each provides a curriculum or database of relevant resources for charting the controversial terrain. In short, each environment provides resources and tools for enhancing both modes of ethics education and inquiry: engagement and detachment.

Case in Point: The Dax Cowart CD-ROM

A Right to Die? The Dax Cowart Case was the first and remains the foremost in a series of interactive multimedia projects conceived under the rubric Project THEORIA. As an acronym, THEORIA stands for "Testing Hypotheses in Ethics: Observation, Realism, Imagination, and Affect." *Theoria* (Greek for *theory*) is also an allusion to the concept of theory rooted in concrete observation. It plays upon the common etymological root of both theory and theater in the ancient Greek verb *theorein*: to see, to view, to behold. Project THEORIA aims to provide a theater for ethical theory, to bring it to ground in observable, palpable, affective contexts that are rich in the complex reality that any competent theory must first behold in order to explain. The aim is to design a theater wherein viewpoints or bias, hypotheses or theories about human values can be challenged by direct observation.

The CD-ROM presents the now classic case of Dax Cowart, a victim of severe burns, blindness, and crippling injuries who persists, under treatment, to insist that he be allowed to discontinue treatment and die. Through interviews with Dax and other principals in the case (his doctors, lawyer, mother, etc.), the user investigates basic ethical issues such as the quality of life, patients' rights and attendant capacities, and the conflicting interests and obligations of medical professionals. Throughout, the user must repeatedly address the central dilemma of whether Dax should be granted his request to die and what reasons should support the decision.

The program will support several hours of interactive exploration of the issues and case material. It allows the viewer to do this in two different modes. The first mode poses questions in the manner of a Socratically guided inquiry by which the user is led carefully to consider the facts, issues, and viewpoints in the case. The program branches and questions users in order to challenge their responses with contrary views and visuals. The program uses these responses to direct the user to other apt or challenging branches of inquiry and to query the consistency of an evolving position. When the viewer is asked to make a final judgment about whether or not Dax should be allowed his request to discontinue treatment and die, striking consequences follow for either choice. When the user exits the program, answers and notes indexed to the issues posed can be printed out for review. The second mode allows the user free access to video archives in which the video segments are organized by major issues and principal characters. This more exploratory mode, unencumbered with questions posed by the program, can be used for review or selective browsing of the case material.

In part because of its engaging subject matter, and in part because of its interactive mode of presentation, the program has been readily adapted to a variety of settings. These have included a nursing department in a community college and an ethics class in the Medical Humanities Program at Dartmouth Medical School (Henderson, 1991) as well as philosophy, rhetoric, writing, and humanities courses at universities. The program has also been used within hospitals and medical schools as an in-service learning resource and in a graduate education school seminar on the design of interactive multimedia learning environments. The program can be used in a number of different ways. It has been used as a stand-alone resource with individual students or small teams of students for sustained investigation of the case study and the issues it presents. The system has been used with a projector both in large classes and seminar groups as a lecture and interactive discussion aid, similar to the use of slide carousels in the classroom (see Henderson, 1991). The videodisc environment has also been used as a case study in multimedia design research and in research studies of the impact and role of emotion in moral reasoning, where it provides a window on how different people reason and learn about complex, emotionally charged moral problems in concrete contexts. The program is thus suited to serve as a vehicle for educational-media research as well as innovative education.

For example, the program has been adapted for research purposes with a mixed audience: professionals enrolled in a Masters Program in Medical Ethics and undergraduate students in a course on Argumentation and Controversy (Petraglia, 1991). The intended audience for the program is broadly postsecondary. The notion is that the program and its content must pass muster in both undergraduate and professional education and the continuum between. The feasibility of this ambition is based on the assumption that visual media generally (film, TV) have a very wide "bandwidth," the ability to communicate meaningfully, albeit variously, with audiences of diverse interests, maturity, and background. But, even if correct, this assumption does not obviate the need to be sensitive to designs that may serve one part of the audience spectrum better than another. For example, the program has done better, all things considered, with faculty and medical professionals than with undergraduate or (young) nursing students. One hypothesis is that the former are more mature methodologically, more able to balance competing hypotheses and conflicting intuitions when confronted with open-ended issues and confounding emotion, and that professionals are more practiced in reflective engagement.

A comprehensive effort to evaluate the impact and educational utility of the program will be very long-term, if only because the modes of use (as a stand-alone resource or as a classroom presentational aid), possible audiences and settings (undergraduate ethics courses, writing courses, graduate or in-service professional courses, media-study programs), and allied tasks (for example, paper assignments, group role-play as an ethics committee, and specific tasks testing the cognitive and affective dimensions of moral learning) are so diverse. Another reason why assessment will be a long march is that there are several research agendas in terms of which to try to understand the program's impact (for example, theories of ethical and cognitive development, gender differences in moral epistemology, and moral controversy and the role of emotions therein). There are decades of work here. And we need follow-on efforts, a series of refinements as well as similar applications in ethics, as vehicles. But the priority of this foray into interactive multimedia for ethics education is to emphasize the *primacy of experience*, to remediate and allow recovery from the abstraction of academic ethics. Merleau-Ponty's observation (1964) applies equally across the broad spectrum of our intended audience, in ethics as in other domains of human inquiry:

> The idea of going straight to the essence of the thing is an inconsistent idea if one thinks about it. What is given is a route, an experience which gradually clarifies itself and proceeds by dialogue with itself and with others.

We have a long way to go to understand the reasoning and learning processes upon which our use of multimedia technology purports to have positive impact. And there is little evidence that anyone has developed – or could develop – ultimately clear, operational objectives or success criteria in the *essentially contested* area of ethics (cf. Gallie, 1968). But my interest here is in the apparent efficacy of visually vivid interactive case studies as one means for inducing a palpable sense of predicament, as I tried to do – and illustrated – in the case of Determined above.

The multimedia case study has two crucial dimensions: visual drama – like a film, and interactivity – unlike film. For example, the most powerful visuals are those of Dax in treatment, where he is shown enduring daily, excruciatingly painful, antiseptic washings, or "tankings," for the third-degree burns covering over two-thirds of his body, which is juxtaposed with a voice-over of Dax speaking calmly and eloquently with his psychiatrist about why he wishes to discontinue treatment and die. At a Dartmouth College conference on Dax's case where this film was shown, one member of the audience called these scenes "ethical pornography." Some might argue that such painfully graphic scenes are a gratuitous appeal to the emotions and are too hard to view, and, hence, that they corrupt the process of "rational" deliberation. *Well*, comes the reply, *Such is life – that is just the point!* How else is one to learn to deal with confounding emotion? I assume, in addition, that without exposure to such scenes and the hard information they convey about the realities of any given patient's predicament, one's deliberations would be inadequately informed. In any case, the discomfort of anyone who would presume to judge Dax's case is a small price to pay for the privilege – a price that Dax himself insists that we pay – and the relevance of affective information and perceptions, as an ethical matter, can hardly be argued, as an empirical matter, without comparative access to the alternatives. The adverse or constructive impact of graphic realities and strong emotional responses on moral reasoning and learning seem suitable and important topics for discussion and investigation; they are not topics that can be discussed in the absence of the relevant experience. Consider: even as I describe these scenes as "painfully graphic," most of my readers can have only vague and detached senses of what that might mean.

By contrast, powerful perceptual and emotional appreciation of Dax's predicament is conveyed by the linear video documentary, *Dax's Case,* which we edited for the original videodisc and the current CD-ROM. What, then, is the advantage or "value added" of the interactivity afforded by the videodisc or CD-ROM program? In the retrospective documentary itself, Dax is our tour guide and we learn immediately that Dax did in fact undergo treatment and survive. Yet one exigency of moral decision-making, an exigency that plagued both Dax and his care givers, is the need to make hard choices under profound and irremediable uncertainty about outcomes or their ultimate evaluation. The interactive program allows us to strategically withhold information about long-term outcomes, to present the retrospective views of both Dax and medical staff as if they are contemporaneous with Dax's treatment, in order to put the viewer in a similar, if vicarious, predicament of uncertainty. For example, if, after interrogating all the principal characters and issues in the case at length, the viewer is finally disposed to let Dax discontinue treatment and die, as he requests, the viewer is shown Dax's life ten years later (where, though blind and without fingers, he is married, with his own business and a tolerably good life). If the viewer is finally disposed to keep Dax in treatment, s/he is then confronted with the most powerful, wrenching scenes of Dax's pain in treatment (which he undergoes several times a day for fourteen months, absent of the knowledge that the duration and intensity of the pain suffered will be *only* for 14 months). In either event, the viewer confronts Dax himself testifying, years afterward, that having established a tolerably meaningful life, he still firmly believes and feels that it was wrong – and would again, and always, be wrong – to force him to undergo such treatment for such reasons against his wishes.

As it turns out, after ten long years of agonizing treatment and rehabilitation, the optimism of Dax's doctors about his potential for recovering a life was vindicated. But other questions remain. Was this optimism justified at the time of his initial treatment? Even if so, would the doctors' optimism justify Dax's treatment against his will? Dax himself testifies, years after his initial recovery, that this vindication serves merely to recapitulate his resentment at having been "forced" to undergo treatment. For the viewer, then, the moral dilemma is not obviated by happy endings. Satisfaction with happy outcomes is relative, and not obviously germane to ethical predicaments, while outcomes – and their evaluation – remain uncertain. The pedagogical stratagem here is to recapitulate the dilemma for the viewer: having previously *felt* the uncertainty but now knowing the outcome, would the viewer decide the case differently if she could make her decision anew?

Many students find that, while they would not change their decision about whether Dax should have been allowed to die, their confidence in their judgment and in their reasons for it has been gravely shaken. Like Determined, they may not change their beliefs, nor is that the point. They begin to suffer wonder, a genuine sense of predicament. As one graduate student of rhetoric put it: *I will never underestimate the painful complexity of such dilemmas again.*

Many other students, even once exposed to either the case narrative or the linear video or the interactive program or the testimony of Dax himself in person – or all four – regird the loins of their original intuition or conviction and seek ways to defend it – per what the "research says" about the robustness of people's opinions and quite contrary to the fondest hopes of would-be educators of unreflective opinion (cf. Young, 1994).

Ergo, there is no "magic bullet" or consummate lever for educating minds, young or old. *A Right to Die? The Dax Cowart Case* is just another tool in the kit bag, one dedicated to *the primacy of experience* as a factor in the movement of minds, however modest.

Conclusion

In the CD-ROM program *A Right to Die? The Dax Cowart Case,* there is no attempt to argue any one moral, ethical, political, or sociological viewpoint. Nor does use of the case study either require or preclude any specific meta-ethical or theoretical orientation that a particular instructor might wish to emphasize or apply (particularism, casuistry, principalism, consequentialism, utilitarianism, deontological theory, etc.). Rather, the interactive multimedia case study is modeled to reflect age-old inquisitorial values exemplified in two narrative analogs: Robert Coles' *The Call of Stories: Teaching and the Moral Imagination* (1989) and J. Anthony Lukas' Pulitzer Prize winning study of the school desegregation controversy in Boston, *Common Ground: A Turbulent Decade in the Lives of Three American Families,* (1985), which views the realities and complexities of its social dilemmas through the eyes of participants and professionals on all sides of the larger social problem. The educational goals of the Dax CD-ROM are basic lessons in moral imagination, in the spirit of the following observations on cognate projects, but with the added impact and reflective opportunity afforded by a medium that is both visual and interactive:

> The three families at the center of my story were not selected as statistical averages or norms. On the contrary, I was drawn to them by a special intensity, an engagement with life, which made them stand out from their social contexts. At first, I thought I read clear moral imperatives in the geometry of their intersecting lives, but the more time I spent with them, the harder it became to assign easy labels of guilt or virtue. The realities of urban America, when seen through the lives of actual city dwellers, proved far more complicated than I imagined.
>
> (Lukas, 1985)

> I try to . . . bring the reader up close, so close that his empathy puts him in the shoes of the characters. You hope when he closes the book his own character is influenced.
>
> (William Carlos Williams, quoted in Coles, 1987).

Likewise, the Dax CD-ROM aspires to bring its audience "up close" to human realities, moral perplexities, and conflicted sensibilities that often confound our best efforts to chart and lead decent human lives. It aims to induce incontestably crucial conditions of competent ethical judgment or theoretic reflection: the vivid representation of the interests of others; the appreciation of moral, emotional and practical straits that, but for fickle fate or feckless imagination, afflict us all – our common human ground for negotiating conflict in community, without which we have only a community in conflict. A third objective is Morrill's *values consciousness:* to bring viewers "up close" to their very own (often inchoate and conflicted) values; to induce the self-knowledge and intimate reflection on one's own sensibilities so often neglected or impossible in abstract academic study, which too often suffers from what Coles (1987) terms *the ever present temptation of the intellect to distance anything and everything from itself through endless generalizations* (one's own values included).

In sum, ethical wisdom is formed in that crucible of moral experience in which ethical hypotheses and ethical theory are ultimately tested. Ethical judgment and ethics education require more than the capacity and opportunity for skilled ratiocination; *inter alia* the vivid representation of the interests of others; practiced confrontation with hard facts, unforeseen consequences, and strong feelings; and active deliberation under the duress of emotion, hard choices, and irreducible uncertainties. Interactive multimedia can simulate these conditions, present both the affecting realities of "real life" situations and the reflective opportunities that should be afforded by academic study, and thereby enhance two essential and complementary modes of ethics education: engagement and detachment.

A Sample Pedagogical Tour for Teachers

This sample tour will provide quick familiarity with the basic features and contents of the program, with some comments on pedagogy. This section is intended for instructors and can be used to give classes a general introduction to the case. Because it discusses pedagogical stratagems and reveals contents of the CD that are best left for discovery by students, we recommend that only the **Overview of the Program** be given to students as an aid for navigating the CD, although we have found that most users require no navigational aid beyond the sequence of program segments that their instructor assigns for viewing.

The basic purpose of the CD is simple: to supplement traditional abstract case narratives or linear video media for presenting case studies to students, not to prescribe a particular program of study. We hope that the interactive video format allows more freedom and motivates greater reflection in the exploration of the complex, concrete realities underlying abstract ethical concerns. Once you are familiar with the basic features and structure of the program, you may wish to systematically explore its content in order to devise uses and sequencing that best serve your own purposes.

1   Starting from the **Main Menu**, select **Archives**. From the Archives, select **Case Chronology**. This section describes the case of Dax Cowart in its traditional textual treatment

Later on, you may wish to compare this summary with the interactive interrogation of "the facts" provided by the **Facts of the Case** under the **Guided Inquiries**. This exercise in narrative analysis is designed simply to sensitize the users to the questions of what facts are relevant and how they should weigh them. The "facts" of the case will take on greater dimension and texture once the users move beyond their narrative representation to the video presentation.

2 Leave the Archives and return to the Main Menu. Select **Guided Inquiries** and then **Medical Professionals' Obligations**.

A The first segment is *Dr. White* (you can get brief profiles of him and others by browsing through the **Principals** in the Archives section). Dr. White begins by speaking about the case and Dax's wish to die.

B When the segment is finished, select **Continue**. We have provided a scale to reflect user responses. The input on this scale determines the context of the next segment. Select a point on the scale and then select **Continue**. The text field can be used to type in a response to the question that is posed. The program does not understand what the user is typing, but it can save this input to a file (under the question) for later retrieval (via a printer). **Commentary** buttons provide prompts to help the user think critically about the selected section.

C The next segment is *Dr. Larson*. Let the sequence run its course. This illustrates an important fact and reality about medical care givers. Dr. Larson's position on whether to keep Dax in treatment is similar to Dr. White's, but the two doctors' attitudes and styles differ markedly. Dax must confront not only arguments but attitudes, a dimension of his reality that is better represented on the CD than in narrative form. In addition, the doctors' attitudes express their capacities and interests as persons, not merely their intellectual or professional convictions. These also are relevant "facts" of the case not so well revealed in narrative form.

3 Select **Main Menu** to leave this branch of inquiry. From the Main Menu select **Archives** and then **Principals**. Select **Dax's Nurse** and then the segment "I can remember the feelings that I had . . . ." This segment reflects yet another attitude of a care giver who could not see her way clear to help Dax die. Notice

that the various medical professionals see and frame the central problem posed by Dax differently, in addition to having different attitudes towards Dax. Is Dax asking them simply to release him from treatment? Or, in effect, to kill him? Or to help him to commit suicide? Does it matter how the question is framed?

When the segment is finished, return to the **Archives: Principals** menu.

4 From here, select **Dax**. Select the segment "What really, I guess, astounds me . . . ". The segment shows Dax in treatment. It also has a voice-over in which he presents one of the arguments for his position. (There are those who might argue that these scenes are an appeal to the emotions and hence irrelevant to the decision-making process. It is one of the contentions of this project that without such scenes/ information, one's decision-making process is ill-informed. Indeed, one might argue that if the only material available is the text, people might not know what the characters in the narrative are talking about. In this case, the technology and the pedagogy go hand-in-hand in making possible the appropriate teaching of this subject matter. These assertions, we believe, have consequences that touch the very core of the curriculum.)

5 Leave this segment and return to the Main Menu. Select **Guided Inquiries** and from there select **Final Position**. This segment demonstrates another advantage of interactive video (this time, over linear video). We have repurposed footage from two films: *Please Let Me Die* and *Dax's Case*. In the latter, Dax is featured in the introduction to the film. The viewer immediately knows that Dax went through his treatment and survived. Yet one of the essential features of moral decision-making is the need to make a hard choice without knowing all the consequences of one's decision. We maintain that reality in this program by having the viewer participate in the decision-making process (by casting his or her vote on whether Dax should get his wish or not). This creates a level of engagement that is not possible in any other medium (short of the actual experience).

6   Choose **Yes** (Dax SHOULD be allowed his request). This will show Dax ten years later – he has a business and is married.

As it turns out, the optimism of Dax's doctors was vindicated. But other questions remain. Was this optimism justified at the time of his initial treatments? Even if so, would the doctors' optimism justify Dax's treatment against his will? Immediately following the scenes of Dax's life after his long recovery, Dax appears to argue that were he to suffer the same plight again "tomorrow," and even if he knew for certain how well things would turn out, it would still be wrong for anyone to "force" him to undergo such a long and painful treatment against his wishes.

For Dax, we learn that this vindication serves merely to recapitulate his condemnation. For the viewer, then, the moral dilemma is unassuaged by happy endings. Satisfaction with happy outcomes is relative. The pedagogical stratagem here is to restate the dilemma for the user: having felt the uncertainty but knowing this outcome, would you decide any differently if you could make your decision anew?

Strategies for Use

Some of the greatest impediments to the success of computer-based learning reside not only in the lack of robust and pedagogically sound software, but in the careful and sensitive use and integration of such software in the classroom. We have tried to address the former problem; it is up to the instructor to manage the latter.

One caveat is: never "throw a disc" at a student. Thoughtful planning and preparation are required before a student uses any software. In what follows we offer some issues to think about and some guidelines to consider.

The user should not be distracted or impeded by the technology itself. The equipment should be conveniently available. Easy access to the software and hardware should be worked out with your library, academic computing or instructional technology department. Technical support staff should also be able to assist in the set up and maintenance of the software and hardware. Clear communication channels should be established to assure that any problems that arise will be known to the instructor as soon as possible.

Just as a new book requires a careful preview, so too should you become familiar with the content of this program. Parts of this manual provide you with a sample tour and a detailed description of the program's content. But unlike a book, it will be important to get some hands-on experience with the actual system.

Here are some logistical and practical questions to think about as you begin to plan for the use of this program:

- What are the school's resources and procedures in regard to the use of computer software and hardware by students in a course?

- Will the CD be on library reserve, in a public computer cluster, or in your office?

- Are there two, ten, or thirty systems for you to use and how will you tailor your use to the allocation of resources?

- How much time would you expect your students to need with the program and how will this be spread over the number and availability of machines?

- Will you use a sign-up procedure and how would you handle students who missed their turn? Would you have a "hidden extension" for the use of the program?

- Check to see that ear phones are available if the equipment is used in a room where others are working.

- How will you monitor student use?

- Do you want the students to evaluate the program? Do you want to evaluate their use of the program?

- The program has the option of recording student responses and notes – how might you incorporate this feature into a class assignment?

There are a number of different ways that this program can be used. Here are some models and suggestions:

1 **Use as a lecture or discussion aid**, interactively, in front of a whole class or seminar. For example, you could illustrate a presentation of the case and issues with relevant segments from the Archives. In effect, the CD can be used as a documentary, but one that can be presented selectively. Segments can be arranged in different sequences to provoke questions or instantly accessed to answer questions. Instant, random access to any video segment is a feature that makes the CD more flexible than a videotape.

Of course, the use of projection equipment adds another level of technology and consequently another set of potential problems (from cables to focus). Until projection devices become a completely natural part of the classroom setting, it will be important to work closely and in advance with those responsible with room assignments and equipment setup. It will also be important to test out the setup prior to the actual class time.

2 **A single student** accessing the CD through a computer is a more typical mode of use for this interactive media. For example, you may assign the Medical Professionals' Obligations in the Guided Inquiries section and limit the assignment to one hour per student. Or you may assign all of the Guided Inquiries and allow the time each student allots to be open-ended. As noted above, you will need to calculate the ratio of machines to students and schedulable time. The time a student will require for complete coverage of all the case material and exercises in the Guided Inquiries varies from two to six hours. Generally, one would use the Guided Inquiries for structured assignments and the Archives for review. But interesting assignments can be made where the student is allowed free, unstructured exploration of the Archives.

Single-person use need not be limited to students in a course within formally prescribed assignments. The CD may be treated like any other generic library resource (such as reference books or films) for independent use on available equipment by members of the community at large.

3 **Collaborative learning in pairs or small groups** can be an effective way for students to think about the issues. It affords another level of interaction by allowing students to discuss options before making selections or typing responses. This mode of use requires an area in which students may talk aloud without disturbing others. Role playing can be incorporated in group assignments to simulate the kinds of collective deliberations required in real world settings, such as hospital ethics committees. Each student might be asked to assume the role of one of a number of committee members (doctor, lawyer, nurse, social worker, ethicist, etc.) and to research the role. Alternatively, the ersatz ethics committee could be evenly divided into those who will represent hospital policy-makers and those who will be patient advocates.

4 **Linked to the World Wide Web**, this case study can be embedded in the larger, on-going discussion about patients' rights and physicians' responsibilities. A number of sites have links to legal cases as well as diverse forums for special interest groups. Carnegie Mellon's Center for the Advancement of Applied Ethics has established a special site for the "Dax Cowart Case," and users can access this site through **http://www.lcl.cmu.edu/CAAE/Home/CAAE.html** or **http://www.routledge.com/routledge/indepth/dax_main.html** (where links to Dax's case can be found).

The Dax Cowart CD-ROM is suitable for use in any of these modes in a variety of courses and disciplines, where exposure to vivid case material for ethical discussion is wanted. Its use need hardly be limited specifically to medical ethics, ethical theory, or even philosophy courses.

In fact, the CD can be and has been used in settings and with audiences as diverse as hospital ethics committees; nursing students; in-service training programs for health care professionals; or with students (graduate or undergraduate) in journalism, law, writing, and rhetoric classes.

Like the documentary films which it incorporates, the content of the CD is atheoretical: it neither presents nor presumes any particular ethical theory, conceptual framework or technical jargon and is therefore adaptable to many different agendas and curricula.

A Right to Die? is designed as a supplement to a course of study, not for instruction in the concepts or topics of medical ethics or philosophy. It is designed simply to present an example of a difficult and classic case study, replete with paradigmatic ethical issues, and to be used in a variety of interactive ways. The instructor is free to supply any additional instructional or conceptual context as well as specific prescriptions for use.

An Overview of the Program for Users

This section provides an overview of the program in its entirety. The program contains its own introductory section, but the outline below may be helpful for gaining an initial orientation to the contents of the CD-ROM.

Initial Screens

After following the **Start-up Instructions** (p. ix), you will see the title screen. Click **Continue** when you are ready to begin the program.

The next screen explains that the program can store your answers in a file if you wish, and asks you if you would like to choose this option. If you select **Yes**, you will be prompted for a file name which will be saved on the hard disk (if you are using the Windows version, the name must consist of no more than eight letters or numbers, with no spaces in between). Be sure that files are being saved to the hard disk and not the CD-ROM (which is read-only). Saved files can be opened with a standard word processor.

Once you have entered a file name (or if you have chosen not to store your answers in a file) and have seen the warning about material contained on the CD-ROM, you will see the **Main Menu** (Figure 1).

From the Main Menu you can access all sections of the program. The program contains a brief **Introduction** to the program itself and to the case; **Guided Inquiries**, in which you will be led though a narrative case summary and then audio-visual material

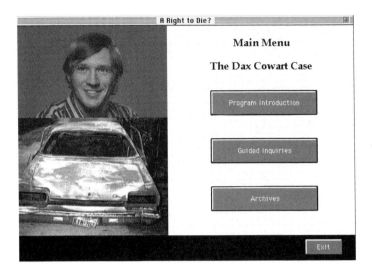

on the issues of the case; and **Archives**, through which you may freely examine the case narrative (all audio-visual case materials are organized under principal characters and issues).

Program Introduction (Main Menu)

The **Program Introduction** consists of **The Basic Question** that will be posed plus an **Overview** of the features and tools contained on the CD-ROM. It is this introductory section that presents you with a charge: to arrive at a reasoned position on whether Dax Cowart should be released from the hospital, in all likelihood to die, as he requests.

Guided Inquiries (Main Menu)

When you select **Guided Inquiries** at the Main Menu, you will see the screen shown in Figure 2.

The Guided Inquiries lead you through the case narrative and the audio-visual material. In the Guided Inquiries you are set the task of coming to a reasoned position on whether Dax should be allowed his request to be released from treatment. Periodically, you are given opportunities to reflect on what you have seen and to affirm or revise your preliminary judgment on whether Dax

Figure 2: The Guided Inquiries Menu

should gain his release. The last section of the Guided Inquiries – **Final Position** – leaves you to make a final judgment. When you have registered your decision, you are presented with a final audio-visual segment to ponder.

The Facts of the Case (Guided Inquiries Menu)

When you select the **Facts of the Case** menu item, you first see your instructions for the task that follows. You are to read a four-paragraph summary of the case and register an initial position as to whether Dax should be allowed his request (Figure 3).

Press **Continue** to read the summary and consider your position, after which you can select the **Initial Position** button to record your view.

Having you take a position at this point is simply a way to engage you in the dilemma and to reveal your initial intuitions on the case, however tentative they may be.

It is assumed that all judgments are tentative, pending further exploration of the case material. Your preliminary position is, in effect, a working hypothesis about what should be done. Although this position can be revised in the course of further

Figure 3:
A Brief
Case
Summary

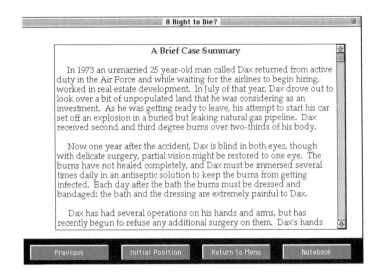

A Right to Die?

A Brief Case Summary

In 1973 an unmarried 25 year-old man called Dax returned from active duty in the Air Force and while waiting for the airlines to begin hiring, worked in real estate development. In July of that year, Dax drove out to look over a bit of unpopulated land that he was considering as an investment. As he was getting ready to leave, his attempt to start his car set off an explosion in a buried but leaking natural gas pipeline. Dax received second and third degree burns over two-thirds of his body.

Now one year after the accident, Dax is blind in both eyes, though with delicate surgery, partial vision might be restored to one eye. The burns have not healed completely, and Dax must be immersed several times daily in an antiseptic solution to keep the burns from getting infected. Each day after the bath the burns must be dressed and bandaged: the bath and the dressing are extremely painful to Dax.

Dax has had several operations on his hands and arms, but has recently begun to refuse any additional surgery on them. Dax's hands

Previous   Initial Position   Return to Menu   Notebook

investigation, there is, given the dilemma presented, no middle ground at this point.

After a preliminary position has been recorded, the program asks about your reasons for taking that position. This again allows you to reflect on your preliminary judgment and motivation for it.

Pressing **Continue** delivers you back to the case summary, this time to consider which particular facts in the summary might support your initial position. This standard task of case analysis is enforced by the following exercise.

You are asked to select sentences in the case summary which state or imply facts that you feel are important to the position you have just taken. For example, suppose that you have just taken the position that **Dax should be allowed his request**. In this context, the sentence "Dax received second and third degree burns over two-thirds of his body" may be important to your position. Double-click one or both of the components of that sentence that will support your position. An asterisk appears in front of all selected facts (Figure 4).

Follow this procedure until you have selected all the sentences and facts (from all four paragraphs of the case summary) that you feel are important to your position.

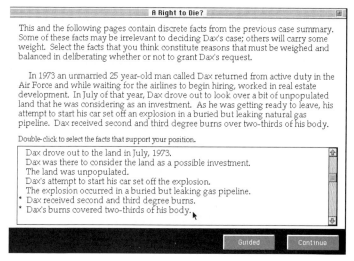

Figure 4:
Selecting
facts to
support your
position

> ▦▦▦▦▦▦▦▦▦▦▦ A Right to Die? ▦▦▦▦▦▦▦▦▦▦ ▣
>
> This and the following pages contain discrete facts from the previous case summary. Some of these facts may be irrelevant to deciding Dax's case; others will carry some weight. Select the facts that you think constitute reasons that must be weighed and balanced in deliberating whether or not to grant Dax's request.
>
>   In 1973 an unmarried 25 year-old man called Dax returned from active duty in the Air Force and while waiting for the airlines to begin hiring, worked in real estate development. In July of that year, Dax drove out to look over a bit of unpopulated land that he was considering as an investment. As he was getting ready to leave, his attempt to start his car set off an explosion in a buried but leaking natural gas pipeline. Dax received second and third degree burns over two-thirds of his body.
>
> Double-click to select the facts that support your position.
>
> Dax drove out to the land in July, 1973.
> Dax was there to consider the land as a possible investment.
> The land was unpopulated.
> Dax's attempt to start his car set off the explosion.
> The explosion occurred in a buried but leaking gas pipeline.
> * Dax received second and third degree burns.
> * Dax's burns covered two-thirds of his body.
>
>   Guided   Continue

The point of this process is to identify significant facts of the case and to begin to reflect on the implications of those bare but pregnant narrative facts. You proceed by rudimentary but crucial steps of case analysis:

1 careful reading of the case summary;
2 formulating a working hypothesis about the case from that reading;
3 considering which sentences in the case summary state or imply facts that seem to support this tentative hypothesis.

Once you have finished selecting facts, the program displays a summary screen (Figure 5).

You are now asked to give a brief explanation of why you chose the particular facts you did.

When you select **Continue**, the program organizes the facts you have chosen under the basic issues of the case (the patient's rights and capacities, the pain of treatment, quality of life issues, and the obligations of the medical professionals). In this manner, the program illustrates simple methods of case analysis: identifying and weighing considerations relevant to a decision in the case.

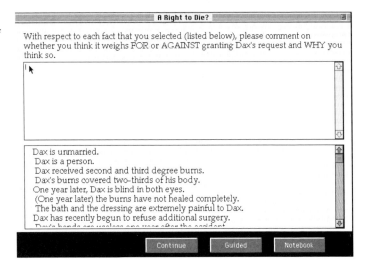

With respect to each fact that you selected (listed below), please comment on whether you think it weighs FOR or AGAINST granting Dax's request and WHY you think so.

Dax is unmarried.
Dax is a person.
Dax received second and third degree burns.
Dax's burns covered two-thirds of his body.
One year later, Dax is blind in both eyes.
(One year later) the burns have not healed completely.
The bath and the dressing are extremely painful to Dax.
Dax has recently begun to refuse additional surgery.

Continue   Guided   Notebook

Having made the point that any study of the ethical issues of a case begins with some thoughtful attention to the facts, the program suggests that you continue to explore the Guided Inquiries related to each of the main issues of the case.

Inquiries into Specific Issues (Guided Inquiries Menu)

The next step in the Guided Inquiries is to explore four sets of issues in Dax's case: **Medical Professionals' Obligations, Pain of Treatment, Quality of Life Issues**, and **Patient's Rights and Capacities**.

If you select Medical Professionals' Obligations from the Guided Inquiries Menu, you will see the screen shown in Figure 6.

The video control bar allows you to pause the movie and replay it at any time. When you have finished listening to Dr. White, you can either **Continue** or select one of the options located at the bottom of the screen. The **Commentary** button contains some thoughts about the content of the doctor's statement. The **Notebook** button will access an on-line wordprocessor for taking random notes at any time during your use of the program.

Figure 6:
Dr. White's
opinion

Assuming you continue the inquiry, you will see the screen shown below (Figure 7).

You are now asked whether you agree with Dr. White that Dax is asking others to participate in his suicide. You are given a scale by which you can record your view: anywhere from "strongly

Figure 7:
Do you
agree with
Dr. White?

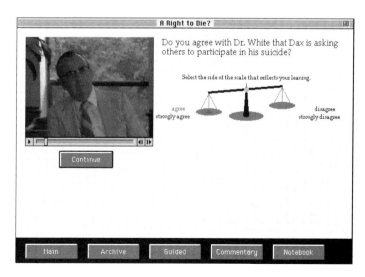

agree" to "strongly disagree". If you wish to review what Dr. White said, you can replay the video at any time.

The final segment in this kind of screen sequence is a **text input field** (Figure 8). Here you are asked to give your reasons for the opinion that you previously registered on the scale. If you had chosen to save your responses, text entered at this point is saved under the question and can be retrieved later as a separate text file.

After you have entered your reasons, press **Continue** to go to the next section in this guided inquiry.

Once you have gone through the **Facts of the Case** and the next four inquiries into specific issues, there is one last task that awaits you: taking a final position, which you do by selecting **Final Position** from the Guided Inquiries Menu.

Figure 8:
The text
input field

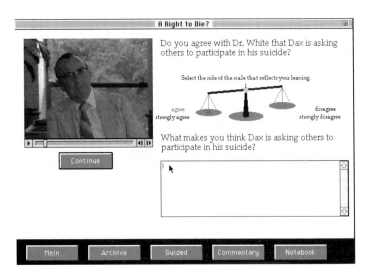

This position is the final one in the sense that you are presented with an "outcome" of this much of Dax's story. The audio-visual material that is presented to you depends on your final position.

The Archives

The **Archives** section of the program allows you to move independently through the case narrative and all the audio-visual material. In the Archives, you may read more details about the case chronology, access the key individuals involved in the case, approach the issues in an open-ended fashion, and note this case's similarity and difference with other famous "right to die" cases (such as Karen Anne Quinlan's case) (Figure 9).

Figure 9:
The
Archives
Menu

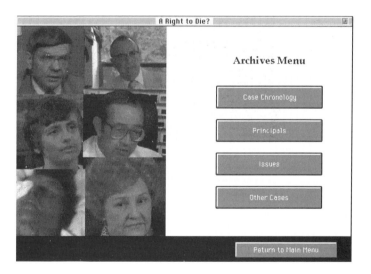

If you select **Principals**, you are delivered to a section of the program which organizes materials according to the principal characters in the case.

By selecting Dr. White, all the audio-visual segments that contain Dr. White are presented, along with a brief profile (Figure 10). Opening transcripts from each segment help you to recap and recall particular evidence while perusing the material.

Notice that here – as in all other sections of the archives – there is no interlocutor: you may observe the footage and take notes, pause and repeat, at your own pace.

Figure 10: Dr. White's perspectives

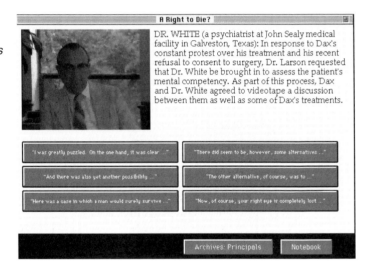

A Narrative Version of Dax's Case

1973: The Accident

Twenty-five years old, handsome, healthy, and recently
discharged from duty as an Air Force fighter pilot, Dax Cowart
has left conflict and danger behind him. He is thinking about the
rest of his life. Contemplating a career in real estate, he takes a
drive into the Texas countryside to look at some land he may
buy. He gets out of the car to walk the length of a boundary line
and gazes across the property, feeling no hint of apprehension.
Nothing tells him this is the last landscape he will ever see.
Nothing warns him, when he slides back into the car and turns
the key, that the spark in his engine will ignite a sea of gas that
has leaked from an underground pipeline. It explodes directly
beneath him, engulfing the entire landscape in flames.

When the flames subside, the blackened shell of Dax's car
remains at the site of the disaster, a silent witness to horror. Its
paint is burned beyond blistering: where it adheres to metal at
all, it clings as fragile bits of ash. The interior is gutted and
charred. One cannot imagine flesh and bone surviving a blast
that has devastated steel, glass, and chrome.

But the explosion, though it blinds Dax and deeply burns most
of his body, does not kill him. Instead, by launching him upon
months of relentless, unspeakable pain, it turns him into a
militant protester. Though he has never before in his vigorous
life had cause to question the principles of the medical
profession, Dax is about to challenge the beliefs and values of all
who render him care after his accident. Like other activists of his
time, he will insist that an individual's rights to dignity and self-

determination override the rights of a system to countermand them even for benevolent reasons. And like many who are dedicated to a cause, Dax will refuse to give quarter to his opponents – though they too have their story.

1974: Dax in Treatment

Dax has been hospitalized for a full year. His face bears no resemblance to the one in earlier photographs. The grinning young pilot is gone, along with the rodeo rider, the crouched quarterback, the handsome high-school senior with the quiet smile. The man in the bed bears their name but wears a new face, transformed in a flash, forever. He cannot see his ravaged features. Though delicate surgery might one day restore some vision to Dax's left eye, it is now sealed beneath a layer of scar tissue, the eyeball moving within the skin like a trapped animal. His right eye is an empty socket covered with gauze. The scars on his chin and throat are dark, disfiguring, and incompletely healed. His lips are swollen and look painfully stretched; they pull slightly away from his teeth, the only visible parts of him not touched by fire.

Worst are Dax's hands, which have been operated on several times. Though doctors feel further surgery might restore some function to both hands, Dax's left hand is now a clenched club at the end of a wasted forearm. The finger segments that remain appear to have been fused by flames. It is as if he wears a tight-fitting mitten of scar tissue over his fist. His right hand is no better. It lies by his side, contorted at the wrist, a gnarl of scars and bone that brings to mind the bound feet of ancient Chinese women.

The rest of Dax's body, too, is covered with terrible, still-raw wounds. Attendants remove the stained dressings daily, while Dax lies immersed in an antiseptic bath. Without these treatments, he will die of massive infections. That, however, is what Dax wants and what he repeatedly demands.

"I don't intend to die from the infection. I would use some other means."

"That is," pursues the psychiatrist with whom he speaks, "you would intend to do away with your own life."

"Yes," Dax says.

Issue: Pain

Dax lies submerged in the antiseptic bath. A thin, pale foam moves lightly upon the surface as the gloved hand of a nurse swirls the solution, bathing Dax's limbs. His knees, bent by scars and burns, rise out of the bath, and the nurse gently removes dressings from his leg. Though the gauze is wet, it sticks to Dax's burns before falling away, stained with blood and pus.

When all the dressings have been removed, the stretcher Dax lies upon like cargo is lifted from the bath by cables and gently tipped to pour off the antiseptic. Attendants wearing masks and gloves swing the stretcher over a table and lower Dax into place. A nurse, also masked and gloved, props his head with a folded towel.

Dax's body, seen full length as it is raised dripping from the bath, looks emaciated. His bent knees are sharp, little more than bone. The tendons behind them are pronounced. His thighs and calves, once shapely and well muscled, are stick-like, wasted by fire and a year of inactivity. His foreleg is the diameter of the nurse's wrist. She applies fresh gauze dressings to his leg with sterile, cotton-tipped swabs, moving slowly and with utmost care, seeming barely to touch his skin at all. But nearly every surface of Dax's limbs have been burned. His skin is covered with mottled, blistery patches, dark and raw in the center with white, peeling layers over and around them. Some areas look thin as parchment; others are marked with a whorled, checkerboard pattern like the singed flesh of a fowl. Dax breathes rapidly, his face contorted, as the nurse applies the dressings. His mouth opens and closes. His burned left eye darts beneath the scars that seal it closed.

Later on, Dr. White, Dax's psychiatrist, asks quietly whether Dax is willing to continue with his treatment just until he gets well enough to act on his own and take his life himself. Dax, who has not recovered enough to do this even after a year of treatment, replies, "Ideally, this would be the best thing to do. If I could go ahead and just see what things are going to be like after I did get out, and if I didn't like them, as you said, terminate my life then. But I don't wish to go through the pain of having my hands and fingers in traction and learning to walk again, which I never had thought of as being a painful thing to do, but, especially with my leg, it's turned out to be *quite* painful."

Dax's burn specialist, Dr. Larson, admits that the treatments he prescribes are painful, but he does not regard pain alone as reason to end them. Larson, a stylish and forceful man, wears his brown, slightly graying hair combed forward to hide a receding hairline. His gray eyes peer through gold-rimmed glasses with a steady, determined gaze, sometimes a glare. His words, when he recalls his determination to continue treating Dax, are forceful, and he is very sure of himself. Though he seems an emotional man, full of passion and commitment, his stated objection to Dax's desire to die is that it is "not reasonable." Larson does not address any other criteria for weighing Dax's demands. He mentions pain, but only, in effect, to dismiss it.

"Don was a very difficult patient to treat," recalls Larson. "In fact, he's the one I remember most. The reason for it is, he made it quite clear, in a very lucid fashion, that he did not want any treatment to be done, and that he wished to be left alone and allowed to die. I felt that this was not a reasonable solution to the problem, and I, in my heart, did not have a difficult time making a decision to treat this man. He had already invested 12 months of one of the most severe emotional and physical drains that anyone could possibly go through. So it was not difficult for me to say, 'You're like a marathon runner that's run 24 miles and you've got one more mile to go to complete the race. Let's stay with it.'"

Though Dax's physicians refuse to stop his treatments, they do respond to his persistent complaints about pain with an effort to reduce it further. Dr. White, the psychiatrist, suggests that perhaps Dax can be persuaded to continue treatment if the dosage of the painkiller is increased. In fact, when Dax finally does receive stronger medication, it seems to help. Dr. White, the psychiatrist says, "Now, just a few days ago you were really pleading to be allowed to leave the hospital and to go home and die. . . . The tubbing each morning was terribly painful and . . .

you thought you could not go on. . . . How do you feel about that now?"

Dax, resting on smooth linens after his daily treatment is over, replies rather incoherently: "The injections that I'm getting now have decreased the pain a whole lot, to where, while I can remember some of what, some things after I get out of the tank and I, uh, wake up from a nap, from under the influence of the drug, I can't . . . I think back, and I can remember being in some pain, but . . . just as soon as they quit I just drop off to sleep again, and so it's not nearly as bad as it was before."

Though Dax, drugged and grateful for relief, remembers little about the pain of his daily baths and dressing changes, he still reels from that pain when it assaults him. Even with heavier doses of drugs in his veins, Dax reacts violently to the least touch during treatment. As his nurses apply new dressings, he cries out repeatedly, pleadingly, with his voice rising, "Easy, easy, hey, easy. Oh, easy, easy. Hey, easy on the back of my leg!" Though the nurses are exquisitely gentle, Dax, both angry and anguished, finally yells, "Oh, GOD!"

Dax, who would end his life because that is the only immediate way to end his pain, is unable to do so because he hasn't the means. He cannot sign the necessary papers, or leave his bed, or walk, or drive, or see. He cannot hold a gun or uncap a bottle of pills and swallow them unaided. Helpless to carry out his wishes on his own, and surrounded by others unwilling to fulfill them, he is compelled to submit to healing.

Issue: Quality Of Life

Despite his medication-induced amnesia and his increased relief after his treatments, Dax stills wishes to die. "If I felt that I could be rehabilitated to where I could walk and do other things normally, I might have a different feeling . . . " Dax explains. "But being blind itself . . . influences my thinking on that. There's no way that I want to go on as . . . blind and a cripple."

Dr. White reviews with Dax the prospects for his future: "Now, of course your right eye is completely lost, and it's unclear at this point how much sight might be restored to the left eye. But it's possible that some degree of useful vision can be restored there, though there's no way to know that until some of the operations are done. Your hands, the surgeons feel, likely can be restored to some degree of reasonable function. That is, where you could pick up things, use a pencil, dress yourself, that sort of thing."

Dax can vividly recall the person he was – the vigorous, adventuresome young man who was shaped over a short lifetime by a complex of influences – his genes, gender, interests, culture, and the time in which he lived. That Dax was changed instantly, but only outwardly, by the random catastrophe that exploded his life. It is clearly difficult for Dax, as he is now, to imagine settling for "some degree of reasonable function." He explains: "I've played golf, surfed, rodeo-ed . . . played football and basketball in school, run track, and I'm very oriented towards athletics in general. And now I think at best I can just be rehabilitated to the extent where I could make it along rather than be able to do the things I really enjoy. If I were enjoying myself after being rehabilitated, I think it would have to be by just changing completely the things that I'm interested in. I don't think that's very likely."

Dax, then, does not wish to suffer the harsh, interminable pain of treatment only to face a life of constraints he believes would be intolerable. Though deep, self-defining impulses – to move, run, compete, train, and strive – still live within him, he can no more act upon them than he can open his scarred left eye and see his altered face. Nor can he see, in his mind's unblinded eye, a future Dax so changed in his internal makeup that he could forgo the very things that made him who he was: the delight in physical action, the daring, control, and strength. The body that once gave him his identity now holds him prisoner in the dark, and the only escape he can imagine is death .

Despite Dax's dire outlook and the severity of his condition, his physiotherapist, Dr. Meier, felt sure – at least in the beginning – that he could help Dax live a useful life. A dark, bearded man in his thirties, he looks back on his approach to Dax's treatment and recalls, rolling his eyes upward, "I wanted to rehabilitate the world, and especially Don Cowart. That wasn't necessarily his priority." The conflict between Meier's professional goals and his patient's wishes eventually penetrated the doctor's certainty. "The difference now," he says, reflecting on Dax's case, "is that

I'm more comfortable with people choosing to not necessarily achieve the level of function that I think is possible for them, especially if it causes them acute discomfort or really may interfere with their quality of life."

Dax's foreboding also fails to dim the optimism of Rex Houston, his attorney and friend, who perceives brightness on Dax's horizon. "I had been talking to Dax about what his future was," Houston says. "After he had the finances to do literally anything he wanted to do, well, I kept impressing upon him that he could in truth do anything he wanted to do. And we talked about him . . . hiring somebody to drive for him, be his eyes, but using *his* brains and *his* know-how to work in real estate."

Houston, who won Dax a large settlement for his injuries, has a point. Dax's physical autonomy, destroyed by his accident, cannot be restored to him by medicine. But might his wealth buy him a measure of it? Won't his quality of life, with all this money, be a good one?

Issue: Patient's Rights And Capacities

"What really astounds me," Dax explains, his voice slightly slurred by the changed shape of his face, "is that in a country like this, where freedom has been stressed so much, and civil liberties in the last few years, . . . a person can be made to stay under a doctor's care and be subjected to treatments, such as the dressing changings, which are very painful, against this person's wishes."

He asks Dr. White why it is that a physician can "decide whether a person lives or dies just because someone's put him under your care as a doctor." He adds, "As long as the patient is willing to be treated, I certainly think the doctor should do everything he could." Dax implies a belief in the converse: that when a patient is *not* willing to be treated, the doctor should cease doing even what is well within his power.

Dr. White, the psychiatrist, echoes Dax's remark. "You feel that you probably should have the legal right to say, 'No, I do not want to be treated.'"

"Yes," Dax replies. "I don't see how anyone else could possibly have this right – *justifiably* have this right."

Dr. Baxter disagrees with Dax's belief that he alone should have the right to choose whether he receives treatment. Baxter is Dax's primary physician, the first to treat him after the explosion. He is middle-aged, with brown hair thinning on top. His face is kind, bespectacled. Wearing a white coat and shirt and a striped tie, he speaks calmly and somewhat slowly, gesturing occasionally with his left hand. He tucks his chin and looks up from beneath his eyelids, his brows lifted. He blinks often, nods, and sometimes hesitates as he speaks. Though his expression is one of sincerity and concern, his words betray no emotion as he recalls his relationship with Dax, whom he calls Donny.

"I responded to Donny's request, or demands, to die, at first rather flippantly. 'Oh, you don't want to do that, Donny.' And, you know, on with the treatment, and I literally ignored his initial request. And at some point, I forget exactly when, he called me in and said that he really did wish to die, wished to get legal consultation and to file the proper brief . . . to make me allow him to die, or to help him die, or send him home where he could commit suicide. . . . And I felt at that point that he was serious about it.

"Up to that point, I had felt that the initial expression of the desire to die, when he came in, could well be not accountable, because during the shock phase, and with all the narcotics, burn patients are incompetent to make such decisions. And I would never, under any circumstances, meet the request at that point in time. Later . . . the nurses and other people were just amazed at the lengths Dax would go to to get what he wanted, to gain control of his environment, to manipulate everyone around him. And to this day, I believe that the vast majority of those requests to discontinue treatment were related to his desire to control that environment."

Dr. White, Dax's psychiatrist, is middle-aged, with thin brown hair and dark-rimmed glasses. As he describes his view of Dax's case, he sits before a window, wearing a light gray suit, white shirt, and gray and brown tie. He discusses his position in tones as quiet and neutral as his clothing. His professionally modulated, soothing voice suggests years of calm, carefully unprovocative exchanges with patients.

Dr. White calls Dax's competence into question. As he discusses Dax's behavior after the initial shock phase, he sounds a jarring note, though his voice remains soothing. "There was . . . another possibility that had to be considered; namely, that some of Dax's angry outbursts were a recurrence of angry little-boy feelings that any person will begin to have after undergoing the incredible ordeal that he had been undergoing."

At the time of Dax's treatment, all of his doctors oppose his demands. Dax's mother, in explaining her own opposition, echoes White and Baxter. Though Mrs. Cowart does not·speak of doubt or conflict when she talks about Dax, her manner shifts noticeably from that of a student repeating a rote lesson to that of a mother in pain.

Dax's mother, wearing a print shirt-dress with a bow at the throat, sits on a chintz sofa in front of an early American spinning wheel. Her light brown hair is short and softly curled, her voice low and quietly Texan. Her legs are crossed, and her hands rest in her lap. "When Donny was saying he did not want to live," says Mrs. Cowart, "I thought his condition was so bad he could not make judgments and decisions about what to do with the rest of his life and whether or not to have treatment. So I didn't worry too much about it at the time." But she *looks* worried as she speaks. Her forehead is creased, her blue-gray eyes restless. She blinks repeatedly.

It is not until Mrs. Cowart talks about her emotions, describing rather than explaining herself, that her words and expression bear each other out. "As a mother, it was hard for me to say that I could give up a child," she says simply. "I don't think that I could ever reach this decision." These two sentences bring her close to tears, deepening the downturned lines at the corners of her mouth. Her sorrow is plain – in her words, her face, the break in her voice. If Dax were "to go home" to die, it would be at his mother's house.

Issue: Medical Professionals' Obligations

Those who treat Dax face a deep dilemma. They feel they have no choice but to treat Dax and cause him pain or to watch him die and live with that moral burden. Clearly, it would be easier for the doctors to cling to admirable professional commitments and abstract principles. It would be easier to diagnose the fury of this suffering patient as a psychological reflex than to admit the depth of his agony, especially when he holds them, the doctors, responsible for its perpetuation. Though inconsistencies, pronouncements, and self-serving interpretations appear in the accounts of Dax's physicians, who would not resort to them? Each of these doctors, unwilling to help Dax die, must justify keeping him alive.

"I was greatly puzzled," says Dr. White. "On the one hand it was clear Dax's yearning to die, his protest of wishing to die, was not the product of mental illness. On the other hand, here was a case in which a man would surely survive, could probably achieve some degree of normalcy in his life, . . . find ways to enjoy life and make something of his own existence, and yet he wanted to die. There was no issue of his having a fatal disease or his being sustained through a comatose period that would never end . . . like Karen Ann Quinlan or such as that. And in essence, he was asking people to participate in his suicide."

Dr. Larson, the burn specialist, admits Dax has gone through "severe" suffering, but he as much as states that his patient's anguish is an investment, to be held until it matures and the profits can be collected. He does not share Dax's view of his pain as an evil to be ended without delay. Instead, Larson becomes angry as he recalls the conflict engendered by his difficult patient.

Larson's anger, though no match for Dax's, comes through when he recalls an encounter he had with Dax. The doctor speaks vehemently, lifting his right palm with the fingers bent and stiff. The gesture is one of mixed passion and frustration. "I went into Don's room and asked him, 'Don, how do you feel today?' He says, 'Leave me alone! I want to die!' And so the attacks started at that time. I said, 'Hey, fellow, if you're half the man I think you are . . . then don't ask us to let you die, because in a sense what that means is that we're killing you.'" Larson, taking Dax's demands as attacks, responds accordingly, with indignation. He seems unable to see beyond the perceived affront.

Larson speaks as if having certain means justifies their use. "I have the knowledge and the means of caring for this patient so that he does survive, and he's asking me not to do this. Why am I in medicine?" Larson's implicit answer is that he is in medicine to save lives, not permit them to end, or be ended, unnecessarily. Instead of taking seriously the question of suffering, and whether it justifies letting go of a life that could be saved, Larson, like Baxter and White, suggests that Dax wait until he can cause his own death.

"If you want to die," Larson remembers saying heatedly to Dax, "then let me fix your hands. Let me go and operate on those hands and at least open them up so you can do something with them. And then if you want to commit suicide . . . you're able to do it. But don't ask us, stand here and ask us to literally kill you. If you want to die, you do it yourself." Dr. Larson does not, by word or gesture, betray any doubt about his position. What comes through most strongly, besides his anger with Dax, is frustration. He has been denied the attempt to open Dax's hands – to do his job. Does his personal stake in Dax's treatment indicate disregard for his patient? Or, paradoxically, do his railing at Dax, his bluntness, and his intense frustration suggest a greater, if clumsier, respect than the other doctors' softer tones convey?

Is Dax really asking others to participate in his suicide? Or is he asking merely that they refrain from their extraordinary, tortuous efforts to heal a body so grievously injured, so ready, in the natural course of things, to die on its own? Would passive acquiescence to this carry the same moral weight as a deliberate act of killing? Does Dax, being helpless, have the right to make others the agents of his death? Though physicians are pledged to ease or eliminate suffering, must Dax's doctors sacrifice their long-term hope for his recovery, and their ultimate goal of preserving life, for the immediate surcease of his pain?

For Leslie Kerr, one of Dax's nurses, these moral questions were made especially difficult by her unmistakable regard for Dax and the fact that he apparently wanted more than her passive cooperation. Looking back, Kerr, who came to know Dax through many long conversations, says, "I can remember the feelings that I had, at thinking, here was a young man that had probably once been very nice looking and very active in his life, and he was now at a point where he wanted not to live and wanted to die. And he was asking me, as a nurse, to either give him something that would allow him to die, or to help him."

Kerr's compassion for Dax, and her ability to acknowledge his pain, are clear. A young woman, probably Dax's age, she is aware not only of the sorrow for which he grieves openly – the destruction of his grace and strength – but also of a sorrow no one else mentions: the loss of his vital good looks.

Though Kerr feels deeply for Dax, she also feels for herself. "I was just out of nursing school, had just graduated, although I had been working at the hospital for a year. I can remember those feelings that I had, at wanting to . . . at feeling, and wanting to help him, but not being able to do that." Ultimately, Kerr is unable to act on compassion alone. She is quick to respond to Dax emotionally, and she feels a pain and helplessness of her own when she must draw the line. Yet she cannot help Dax die. She is, after all, just out of nursing school, still close to the training that deeply ingrains the goal of preserving life. She is also, being new to her profession, perhaps a novice at subduing her emotions in the service of her work. If both these things are true, Kerr is caught between a professional standard and a personal sensitivity. Her actions are dictated by the former, her feelings by the latter.

Dr. Baxter shakes his head as though he is perplexed to this day by the Dax dilemma. "I have felt, though, that it is my obligation to deliver those techniques and services and things that we have been endowed with, to know how to do, to the best of my ability. It is not my decision, whether they work or don't work in an individual case."

Two of Dax's physicians saw one possible way to resolve the dilemma. Both Dr. White and Dr. Larson felt that the standards and obligations of medicine could be satisfied by treating Dax until he no longer had to depend on others to act for him. At that point, Dax could satisfy his own desires. Dr. White explains, "There did seem to be, however, some alternatives that could be considered. One, of course, was to try and help the patient to accept the possibility of going on with his treatment until he was physically ready to leave the hospital and sufficiently able to move about and do things for himself that if he then wished to end his life he could."

Dr. White asks Dax, "Do you have any willingness to wait and see, so at least you would be able to be up and around sufficiently, to handle things with your hands sufficiently, that if at that point you simply did not want to go on with your life, that you would be in a position to terminate it if you wished? Because as it is now, you would be bedfast and would be hard put to do away with yourself even if you were strongly inclined to do so."

Dax responds, "To me, I feel the chances are so small that the pain . . . the end result isn't worth the pain involved to get to the point where I could try it out. Ideally, this would be the best thing to do, if I could go ahead and just see what things are going to be like after I did get out, and if I didn't like them, as you said, terminate my life then. But I don't wish to go through the pain."

1984: The Outcome

Dax is in a dark hallway, moving with a limp toward a square of sunlight in a door at the end. His hand, in silhouette against the window, is still a club. When he opens the door, which he does by turning the knob between his two wrists, he is as blind in the streaming light as in the darkness of the hall.

It has been ten years since Dax was forced to undergo treatment for his crippling disfiguring burns. The pain that made him want to die is gone, but the constraints he feared are not. He is permanently disabled and blind. He lives without possibility of parole from his darkness and incapacities. And the years immediately following his release from the hospital were filled with struggle. He had, on several occasions, attempted suicide. He was also plagued by bouts of insomnia that have, gratefully, subsided.

But Dax, letting his Doberman bound into the house, is cheerful. "C'mere, c'mon in here," he says affectionately to his dog. "You want to go for a walk? You want to go for a walk? *Come* on, *come* on." The dog is giddy, exuberant, a healthy, muscular animal who leaps joyfully at his master.

Dax and the dog turn back down the hall, and Dax feels his way along the wall to a brightly sunlit living room. The furnishings speak quietly of a comfortable middle-class life: plush, wall-to-wall carpet, wood paneling, a lacquered Chinese armoire with raised gold figures, a huge window facing a back yard with a picnic table. Dax sits down next to the dog, talking to him, petting him, and once again using his wrists rather than his club-like hands to guide a chain collar over the dog's head.

Dax's life appears full. He is busy every day with his investments, which he manages from a specially equipped office. Because his hands are of little use to him, he operates an adding machine by punching the keys with his tongue. A computerized voice recites the numbers he has entered and gives him the results of his calculations.

Dax is informally dressed for business in a white jacket, blue shirt, and jeans. His office is full of light, as cheerful as if he could see it. His secretary comes in with a letter for him to sign, and Dax slides a pen through a narrow hole formed in his fused fist by his thumb and finger stubs. His secretary guides his hand to the closing of the letter, and he scrawls D-A-X.

Later, in a restaurant with a friend, Dax requires a similar orientation to the food on his plate. Once he knows where everything is, he holds his fork as he did his pen, much as an unpracticed child holds eating and writing implements. He is able to eat unassisted.

Dax sits in his yard in the sun. The skin around both of his eyes has been opened up, and at first glance his blue eyes appear to gaze intently ahead. But his eyes are fixed, and he never blinks as he speaks. These are artificial eyes. The left one, which had been sealed closed by scars, is surrounded by darkened skin, giving it a sunken look. His face is badly scarred. The skin everywhere has varying textures of scar tissue, shiny and smooth in some places, webbed with tiny wrinkles elsewhere. His lips are still swollen but have healed and no longer look painful. His eyebrows are sparse, or perhaps they have never grown back at all.

Sitting next to Dax in the sun is his wife, Karen, a woman he had lost touch with after a high school acquaintance sixteen years earlier. They met by chance in 1982, after Dax had been living alone in his house for about a year. He and Karen started going out together and eventually fell in love. They have been married for over a year.

Ironically, in Dax's life, nearly everyone's predictions have come true. Dax, as his lawyer anticipated, is not only financially well off but also successful. He is blind and just as disabled as he himself foresaw, and yet, as his doctors assured him, he has recovered sufficiently to function well and live without pain. The only entirely disproven prediction is Dax's own: that he would not be able to enjoy his life amid the constraints of blindness and disability. In this matter, where he and his doctors were irreconcilably opposed in their views, he has been refuted and his doctors' optimism upheld.

Dax, though, has the last words: "If the same thing were to occur tomorrow, and knowing that I could reach this point, I would still not want to be forced to undergo the pain and agony that I had to undergo to be alive now. I would want that choice to lie entirely with myself and no others."

1994: Postscript

The turns in Dax's life since 1984 underscore the uncertainties of human life at large. After finding Karen again and marrying against all expectations, it came to pass that Dax and Karen divorced. However, in 1987 Dax met Randi, a nurse familiar with his by-then famous case. Dax and Randi fell in love, married, and remain happily married today.

Despite initial difficulties, Dax eventually finished law school, passed the Texas bar, and began a law practice, specializing in patients'-rights issues. In time, the law practice gave way to lectures on his case and patients' rights, and he remains adamant, despite the tolerably good life he now enjoys, that it was wrong that he was forced to undergo treatment against his will. This seeming paradox replicates the dilemma that originally confronted Dax and his care givers.

In the years since his accident, two documentaries have been made about Dax's case. The first, *Please Let Me Die!* (1974) was shot at the time of his treatment. A second, *Dax's Case* (1985), added extensively to the first and contains interviews with hospital staff as well as family and friends. In 1989 an interactive videodisc case study, *A Right to Die? The Case of Dax Cowart*, was published as a precursor to the present CD-ROM.

Today, Dax is once again practicing law and is writing his own book about his case. The Center for the Advancement of Applied Ethics at Carnegie Mellon has provided Dax with a multimedia computer that allows him to communicate by electronic voice and video mail over the World Wide Web. Dax, and Dax's case, continue to form the basis for lively discussion and principled disagreement.

Further Annotated Resources

The following resources are even more selective than the references in our **Select Bibliography**, but are classified and annotated suggestions for instructors who might wish to supplement the Dax Cowart CD-ROM for various courses of study. The annotations are intended to help instructors inform, design, or reinforce their own educational strategies and pedagogical tactics in deploying the CD.

Film/Video Documentaries on Dax's Case

The Dax Cowart CD-ROM contains video material edited from the documentary videos *Dax's Case* (1985) and *Please Let Me Die!* (1974), referenced below. It might be of interest for instructors simply to show either or both documentaries in total, in addition to using the interactive CD, or comparatively to employ different modes of presentation of the case study: interactive multimedia (the CD-ROM program), linear video (either of the documentaries below), and narrative text (for example, the version contained in this *Teacher's Guide*, the chronicle contained in Kliever, 1989, or the summary in White and Englehardt, 1975).

Choice in Dying, with Keith Burton and Don Pasquella, *Dax's Case* (film and videotape), New York, NY, 1985. This approximately hour-long production contains retrospective interviews with Dax, his mother, lawyer, best friend, and various care givers filmed ten years after the treatment he protested, as well as scenes from the 1974 film *Please Let Me Die!* (see Kliever, 1989, pp. xv–xvii). This material was edited for purposes of the Dax Cowart CD-ROM. For those wishing to view the full, original, linear video, it is available from Choice in Dying, 200 Varick Street, New York, NY 10014 (1-800-989-9455).

Robert B. White, *Please Let Me Die!* (videotape), University of Texas Medical Branch, Galveston, 1974. This approximately thirty-minute documentary, the first on Dax Cowart while he was in treatment, is available, with an epilogue, from PO Box 555, Henderson, TX 75653.

Discussions of Dax's Case

The following resources provide opportunity for amplifying students' analytic, theoretic and methodologic perspectives beyond the express (and relatively "commonsensical" and theoretically neutral) inquisitorial content of the Dax Cowart CD-ROM. One strategy for motivating a course in moral reasoning or ethical theory might be to begin with an intensive case study, such as Dax's case as presented on the CD-ROM, supplemented by resources such as the following, but first allowing students to induce theoretic and methodologic issues from attention to the details of the striking and pregnant CD-ROM case study.

Tom L. Beauchamp and Lawrence B. McCullough, *Medical Ethics: The Moral Responsibilities of Physicians* (Englewood Cliffs, NJ: Prentice-Hall, 1984). Chapter 4, "Medical Paternalism," provides a summary of the Dax Cowart case and uses it to illustrate in fine detail issues regarding the justifiability of medical paternalism, associated principles of beneficence and autonomy, physicians' responsibilities, patients' rights, and factors that constitute or compromise patients' capacities to make competent and autonomous decisions. A very apt analysis for the study of Dax's case, for an appreciation of the ethical, conceptual, and practical problems such cases pose, and for illustration of ethical reasoning as a delicate weighing and balancing of competing principles (such as "autonomy" and "beneficence") and considerations (such as constitute "competence," "autonomy," or their impairment). This chapter is a cognate analysis of the meanings of autonomy and the justifiability of paternalism (or justifiable medical intervention in the ostensible absence of consent) to "'Who Is the Doctor to Decide Whether a Person

Lives or Dies?' Reflections on Dax's Case" by Childress and Campbell in Kliever, 1989, below. See also chapters 1 and 2 of James Childress, *Priorities in Biomedical Ethics* (Philadelphia, PA: Westminster Press, 1981).

Robert A. Burt, *Taking Care of Strangers: The Rule of Law in Doctor–Patient Relations* (New York: The Free Press, 1979). Chapter 1, "David G and Self-Rule," is a pseudonymous analysis of the Dax Cowart case based on the conversation between Dax Cowart and Dr. Robert B. White, Dax's psychiatrist, which transpires in the 1974 film produced by Dr. White on Dax's behalf, *Please Let Me Die!* The Appendix contains a transcript of this interview. Throughout, the pseudonym "David G" is used to respect and protect Dax Cowart's privacy in order not to usurp Dax's decision to make his case public.

C. E. Harris, Jr., *Applying Moral Theories* (Belmont, CA: Wadsworth, 1986). Chapter 1, "What Is Ethics?," briefly describes the Dax Cowart case pseudonymously and typifies a brief textbook case abstract. Dax's case is also briefly alluded to in James Rachels' article, "Euthanasia," in Tom Regan (ed.), *Matters of Life and Death* (Philadelphia: Temple University Press, 1980).

Lonnie D. Kliever (ed.), *Dax's Case: Essays in Medical Ethics and Human Meaning* (Dallas, TX: Southern Methodist University Press, 1989). Conceived as a companion volume to the 1985 documentary film *Dax's Case* (above), this anthology provides a multi-perspectival case study in its own right. The essays in this volume chronicle Dax's predicament and medical treatment and represent a compelling range of professional and theoretical perspectives on both the specific dilemmas and broader issues that afflicted Dax, his loved ones, and care givers. The volume stands on its own as a collection of essays on fundamental quandaries of medical ethics and the meaning of life *in extremis*, "provocative meditations on human life at the edges of endurance and the limits of hope." Useful companions to this anthology are the review essay by Twiss (1995) and the analysis of Dax's case by Lauritzen (1996), which refer directly to essays in this volume. Kliever's anthology remains the most compendious resource on Dax's case and includes the following contributions:

Keith Burton, "A Chronicle: Dax's Case As It Happened."

Robert B. White, "A Memoir: Dax's Case Twelve Years Later."

James F. Childress and Courtney C. Campbell, "'Who Is a Doctor to Decide Whether a Person Lives or Dies?' Reflections on Dax's Case."

Richard M. Zaner, "Failed or Ongoing Dialogue? Dax's Case."

Joanne Lynn, "Dax's Case: Management Issues in Medicine."

H. Tristram Englehardt, Jr., "Freedom vs. Best Interest: A Conflict at the Roots of Health Care."

Patricia A. King, "Dax's Case: Implications for the Legal Profession."

William J. Winslade, "Taken to the Limits: Pain, Identity, and Self-Transformation."

William F. May, "Dealing with Catastrophe." (See also May's *The Patient's Ordeal*, 1991, below, and its review in Twiss, 1995, below.)

Sally Gadow, "Remembered in the Body: Pain and Moral Uncertainty."

Stanley Johannesen, "On Why We Should Not Agree with Dax."

Lonnie Kliever, "Dax and Job: The Refusal of Redemptive Suffering."

Paul Lauritzen, "Ethics and Experience: The Case of the Curious Response," *Hastings Center Report*, January/February 1996. The utility of the Dax Cowart CD-ROM is predicated upon various assumptions about the value of emotional and experiential appeal or engagement, as articulated in **A Rationale for this Interactive Multimedia Case Study**. This protreptic, or "rationale," is not to be confused with a complete "theory" of the role of either appeal to emotion or appeal to experience in ethical theory or reasoning; it relies rather on "commonsensical" and (somewhat circularly) "experiential" observations about the indispensability of appeals to emotion and experience in ethical deliberation and theorizing. The minimal utility of the CD-ROM and such appeals is to make people "think twice" about their particular judgments, principles, or general approach regarding such cases and issues. Lauritzen's essay provides a preliminary but incisive philosophic address to questions such as: What is *the nature* of appeal to experience in moral deliberation? What is *the role* of appeal to experience in moral deliberation? (Cognate questions concern the nature and role of appeal to experience in ethical theorizing.) Lauritzen's essay on these epistemological and methodological issues are of particular interest because he illustrates his analysis by reference to Dax's case and his critiques of two essays on Dax's case in Kliever (1989), above (Childress and Campbell's as compared with May's perspective). Lauritzen expressly raises these methodological issues and suggests Rawls' notion of "reflective equilibrium" as useful for understanding the dialectic between "appeals to experience" and the testing of ethical judgments, principles, and theory. In short, Lauritzen articulates the dialectical function of appeals to experience underlying our own rationale for the Dax Cowart CD-ROM, which is just one of several modalities for presenting the "stories" of Dax Cowart and other principals in Dax's case. Lauritzen's essay is the more valuable for indicating the bias in the video documentary, *Dax's Case,* from which the video segments of the Dax CD are edited: the video material more thoroughly and compellingly tells Dax's story than the stories of the other principals. This creates a challenge for viewers: to imaginatively elaborate and identify with the "stories" of the other principals. For this reason (Lauritzen's identification of the narrative or experiential shortcomings of the otherwise visually impactful "story" told by the video material), his essay is perhaps the most crucial Dax-relevant resource with which to supplement the use of the Dax Cowart CD-ROM.

William F. May, *The Patient's Ordeal* (Bloomington, IN: Indiana University Press, 1991. The first chapter of this case-based treatise on the ethic of care concerns the Dax Cowart case and is similar to May's essay on Dax's case in Kliever (1989), above. However, this book elaborates in more detail, with further paradigmatic case studies, the ethic of care. See Twiss (1995), below, for an incisive review essay on May's version of the ethic of care as compared with two other moral-theoretic approaches pertinent to Dax's case and medical ethics, as elaborated in essays in Kliever (1989), above: the ethic of liberal individualism and the ethic of the communal good. For a comparative assessment of May's approach, see also Lauritzen (1996), above.

Stanley B. Troup, "Dax's Case," *Journal of the American Medical Association* 262: 18 (November 10, 1989). A review of Lonnie D. Kliever (ed.), *Dax's Case: Essays in Medical Ethics and Human Meaning* (Dallas, TX: Southern Methodist University Press, 1989).

Sumner B. Twiss, "Alternative Approaches to Patient and Family Medical Ethics: Review and Assessment," *Religious Studies Review* 21: 4 (October 1995). Encompassing Lonnie D. Kliever (ed.), *Dax's Case: Essays in Medical Ethics and Human Meaning* (Dallas, TX: Southern Methodist University Press, 1989) and William F. May, *The Patient's Ordeal* (Bloomington, IN: Indiana University Press, 1991), this review essay is more than a book review. Twiss provides an incisive analysis of both the several viewpoints of the Kliever anthology and also a judicious assessment of three broad moral frameworks into which these several perspectives can be clustered: the ethic of liberal individualism, the ethic of the communal good, and the ethic of care. His review of the May volume examines in more critical detail May's approach to the ethic of care (in which the Dax case is one of several paradigmatic cases discussed by May). Twiss' review essay would be valuable companion reading to the Kliever anthology, or by itself, for purposes of raising theoretical and meta-ethical issues and deepening, or giving further direction to, the relatively a-theoretic approach provided by the CD-ROM program.

Robert B. White and H. Tristram Englehardt, Jr., "A Demand to Die," *Hastings Center Report*, June 1975. A summary of the Dax Cowart case followed by two brief but sensitive and incisive essays: one by Dr. White, Dax's psychiatrist and a Professor of Psychiatry at the University of Texas Medical Branch, and one by Dr. Englehardt, a Professor of the Philosophy of Medicine at the University of Texas Medical Branch.

Educational Uses of Dax's Case

The following resources articulate the observations, educational strategies, and pedagogical tactics employed by educators who have employed the Dax Cowart case in one form or another.

Joseph Henderson, *The Use of Interactive Video in an Ethics Class with First-Year Medical Students* (Hanover, NH: Interactive Media Lab, Dartmouth Medical School, 1991). This videotape illustrates the interactive use of the prototype videodisc on Dax's case to motivate and inform discussion of the case and issues with a large class of first-year medical students at Dartmouth's medical school. Dr. Henderson and his staff designed the first Macintosh™/Hypercard™ program to drive the prototype videodisc version of *A Right to Die?*

Joseph Petraglia, *Exploring the Effects of Realism on Arousal and Rhetorical Representation* (Pittsburgh, PA: Carnegie Mellon University, 1991). A doctoral dissertation in English/Rhetoric that utilized a tailored version of an early interactive videodisc presentation of the Dax Cowart case to test hypotheses about the effects of realistic, visually rich, and engaging case material on affective arousal and, in turn, on university students' perceptions of salient issues in the case study. This study suggests interesting trade-offs between two venerable pedagogical values: "objectivity" of critical judgment and "realism" in the presentation of controversial subject matter.

William Steele, "Lives in the Balance," *Cornell Alumni News*, February 1983. An engaging and poignant description of an annual conference of Cornell University's Program on Law, Ethics, and Religion devoted to the Dax Cowart case. Participants first read the transcript of an interview with Dax Cowart from 1974, then viewed the 1974 film in which this interview occurred during Dax's painful burn treatments, and finally convened for a discussion and role-plays with Dax Cowart himself. The distinct impacts of the transcript, the film, and the subsequent interactions with Dax himself on the participating attorneys provide telling answers to the author's question: *What would participants gain from an experience such as this that they wouldn't learn in the classroom?*

Richard Young, "Toward an Adequate Pedagogy for Rhetorical Argumentation: A Case Study in Invention," presented at the Third International Conference on Argumentation, University of Amsterdam, June 21–24, 1994. This lecture discussed the results of a concerted attempt to test and quantify the effects of using the original interactive videodisc version of the Dax Cowart case in a course on controversy and argumentation at Carnegie Mellon University. The difficulty of quantifying such effects is discussed, as well as the equally frustrating difficulties in qualitative evaluation of the effects of the case study as presented in various media (narrative, linear video, and interactive multimedia). This lecture stands as a signal caveat either to those who might presume that advanced or fancy technology can solve perennial educational problems, or to those who might suppose that traditional, non-fancy or a-technological means to any educational goal are superior by virtue of being less opaque in their utility. Basically, Young's essay is a lesson in humility for all would-be pedagogues: with or without the aid of technology of any description, how shall we construe or document our presumptions to "success" in education?

Ethical Analysis and Theory

Tom L. Beauchamp and James F. Childress, *Principles of Biomedical Ethics*, Fourth Edition (New York: Oxford University Press, 1994). A classic text on biomedical ethics, presumably representative of the methodology known as "principalism." For a critical perspective on "principalism" and the evolution of this approach through the several editions of the classic Beauchamp and Childress text, see the review of the fourth edition by Ezekiel J. Emanuel, "The Beginning of the End of Principalism," *Hastings Center Report*, July/August 1995.

Rebecca Dresser and Peter J. Whitehouse, "The Incompetent Patient on the Slippery Slope," *Hastings Center Report*, July/August 1994. While dealing with cases of incompetent patients, ostensibly unlike that of Dax Cowart, this illuminating article tackles the problem of defining "objective standards" for evaluating a patient's interests, experience and quality of life, a problem that also afflicts cases where medical professionals and presumably competent patients differ in their assessments of the value of medical interventions.

Bernard Gert, *Morality* (Oxford University Press, 1988). This treatise is a prodigious effort at articulating a concertedly systematic moral theory, in ostensible contrast to the approaches to ethical issues nominated "particularism," "casuistry," or "principalism." Some viewers presume that the Dax CD is committed to one of these a-theoretic approaches to ethical issues. This is simply not the case; but we recognize the propensity to confusion. For instructors who wish to illustrate – and challenge their students with – the effort to give a full-blown theoretic account of case-based ethical judgment or analysis, particularly in the domain of medical ethics (for which Dax's case provides a prime opportunity), Gert's treatise is exemplary. See, especially, the discussion of biomedical issues in Chapter 14, which illustrates the concrete and methodical application of his exemplary rigorous moral system in this salient domain.

Matthew Hanser, "Why Are Killing and Letting Die Wrong?" *Philosophy & Public Affairs*, Vol. 24, No. 3, Summer 1995. In the voluminous literature on the putative and arguable distinction between killing and letting die, this very recent essay is a convenient place to start, from which one can work backwards to investigate the purview of the classic literature and the archeology of the problem.

Albert Jonsen and Stephen Toulmin, *The Abuse of Casuistry: A History of Moral Reasoning* (University of California Press, 1988). See especially the discussion on theory and practice in Chapter 2 and the model of casuistical reasoning in Chapter 16. Resort to the detail and drama of cases such as Dax Cowart's, especially in video format with relatively a-theoretic content, is often presumed to presuppose or recommend a "particularist" or "casuistical" or otherwise a-theoretic approach to ethical issues. Such is not the case: the utility or necessity of "getting down to cases" in ethics does not preclude any particular methodological, meta-ethical, or theoretical commitment. However, for an understanding of the history and methodological commitments of the approach to ethical reasoning nominated generally as "casuistry," Jonsen and Toulmin's study surely rewards close study.

Alan Meisel, *The Right to Die*, Volumes I and II, Second Edition (New York: John Wiley & Sons, 1995). A compendious treatment of the legal status and jurisprudential issues regarding the right to die, as well as the medical, psychiatric, ethical, and philosophic aspects. For issues especially pertinent to the Dax Cowart case (a case of a putatively psychiatrically certified "competent" patient who wished to refuse treatment and die), see especially Volume I; in particular: Chapter 1, "What Is the Right to Die?; Chapter 2, "Nature and Sources of the Right to Die"; Chapter 3, "Basic Principles for Medical Decisionmaking"; Chapter 4, "Meaning and Effect of Incompetence"; and Chapter 8, "Limitations on the Right to Die."

E. Haavi Morreim, "Profoundly Diminished Life: The Casualties of Coercion," *Hastings Center Report*, January/February 1994. An examination of seemingly intractable conflicts of belief about the value of life and the question "How best to preserve freedom for each party to honor its values without coopting unwilling others." This article deals with converse cases to that of Dax Cowart, cases where the physician seeks to terminate treatment against a patient's or a family's wishes. But it illustrates why "solutions" which deny the depth of a value conflict are no solutions at all. This article's conflict-resolution sensitivity to apparently opposed values would be instructive to those who are tempted to finesse any of the moral dilemmas underlying Dax's case or the like.

Roles of Emotion in Ethical Reasoning

The deliberate use of vivid case material such as Dax Cowart's case in ethical education or inquiry, whether through textual narrative or audio-visual media, might appear to presuppose that emotional arousal and engagement can provide useful, appropriate, or even essential effects, perspective, perceptions, capabilities, data, or information. While respecting the controversiality of such presuppositions and the ostensible incompatibility between emotion and reason, the following resources provide analyses of quintessentially moral sentiments and various views of the constructive roles of sensibility and emotion in moral life and thinking. The role of emotion, whether for better or worse, is, in any case, an important issue for educational strategies and pedagogy that trade in realistic case studies or vivid thought experiments. The following is a highly selective sample of salient and germane literature.

Mark Johnson, *Moral Imagination: Implications of Cognitive Science for Ethics* (Chicago: University of Chicago Press, 1993). See especially Chapter 8 on the roles of narrative and empathetic imagination in moral reasoning.

Paul Lauritzen, "Ethics and Experience: The Case of the Curious Response," *Hastings Center Report*, January/February 1996. (See comments, above, under **Discussions of Dax's Case**.)

Martha Nussbaum, "Compassion: The Basic Social Emotion," *Social Philosophy & Policy*, Winter 1996, and *Love's Knowledge* (New York: Oxford University Press, 1990). See especially Chapter 2, "The Discernment of Perception."

Richard Rorty, *Contingency, Irony, and Solidarity* (Cambridge University Press, 1989). A signal insight of Rorty's pragmatism is consonant with the design and intended use of the Dax CD-ROM, that either perceiving a moral problem, or making an ethical judgment, or theorizing about ethics is – at bottom and ineluctably – a matter of the *imaginative identification with the details of others' lives.*

Public Reason and Moral Reason

Recent meta-ethical approaches to applied ethics have elaborated the "conversational turn" in moral argument. Key figures in this area include Habermas, Putnam, and Rawls. The emphasis here includes widening "reflective equilibrium" by embedding empathy and detailed reciprocity into moral reflection and by placing the deliberative process within the intelligent conduct of communal inquiry.

Jürgen Habermas, "Discourse Ethics," in *Moral Consciousness and Communicative Action* (Boston: MIT Press, 1990) and "Remarks on Discourse Ethics," in *Justification and Application* (Boston: MIT Press, 1993).

Hilary Putnam, "How Not To Solve Ethical Problems," in *Reason With a Human Face* (Boston: Harvard University Press, 1990) and "A Reconsideration of Deweyan Democracy," in *Renewing Philosophy* (Boston: Harvard University Press, 1992).

John Rawls, *Political Liberalism* (New York: Columbia University Press, 1993).

See also the Special Issue of *The Journal of Philosophy* (Vol. XCII, No. 3, March 1995): "Reconciliation through the Public Use of Reason: Remarks on John Rawls's *Political Liberalism*" by Jürgen Habermas and "Reply to Habermas" by John Rawls.

Select Bibliography

The following is an alphabetical listing of the resources that are referenced in either the text of this *Teacher's Guide* or the specific section on **Further Annotated Resources.**

Baier, Annette. *Postures of the Mind: Essays on Mind and Morals* (Minneapolis: University of Minnesota Press, 1985).

Beauchamp, Tom L. and James F. Childress. *Principles of Biomedical Ethics*, Fourth Edition (New York: Oxford University Press, 1994).

Beauchamp, Tom L. and Lawrence B. McCullough. *Medical Ethics: The Moral Responsibilities of Physicians* (Englewood Cliffs, NJ: Prentice-Hall, 1984).

Bok, Derek. "Looking into Education's High-Tech Future," *EDUCOM Bulletin*, Fall 1985.

Burt, Robert A. *Taking Care of Strangers: The Rule of Law in Doctor–Patient Relations* (New York: The Free Press, 1979).

Callahan, Sidney. "The Role of Emotion in Ethical Decisionmaking," *Hastings Center Report*, June/July 1988.

Childress, James. *Priorities in Biomedical Ethics* (Philadelphia, PA: Westminster Press, 1981).

Choice in Dying, with Keith Burton and Don Pasquella. *Dax's Case*. Film and videotape (New York: Choice in Dying, 1985).

Clark, Richard. "Reconsidering Research on Learning from Media," *Review of Educational Research*, 53, 1983.

Coles, Robert. "Moral and Social Inquiry Through Fiction," *New York Times Book Review*, October 25, 1987.

Coles, Robert. *The Call of Stories: Teaching and the Moral Imagination* (Boston: Houghton Mifflin, 1989).

Dresser, Rebecca and Peter J. Whitehouse. "The Incompetent Patient on the Slippery Slope," *Hastings Center Report*, July/August 1994.

Elliott, Carl. "Where Ethics Comes from and What to Do about It," *Hastings Center Report*, July/August 1992.

Frank, Robert. *Passion Within Reason: The Strategic Role of the Emotions* (New York: W. W. Norton, 1988).

Frankfurt, Harry G. *The Importance of What We Care About: Philosophical Essays* (Cambridge: Cambridge University Press, 1988).

Fullinwider, Robert. "Learning Morality," *Report from the Institute for Philosophy & Public Policy*, Spring 1988.

Gallie, W. B. "Essentially Contested Concepts," *Philosophy and the Historical Understanding*, Second Edition (New York: Schocken Books, 1968).

Gert, Bernard. *Morality* (Oxford University Press, 1988).

Gordon, Robert M. *The Structure of the Emotions: Investigations in Cognitive Philosophy* (Cambridge: Cambridge University Press, 1987).

Habermas, Jürgen. *Moral Consciousness and Communicative Action* (Boston: MIT Press, 1990).

—— *Justification and Application* (Boston: MIT Press, 1993).

—— "Reconciliation through the Public Use of Reason: Remarks on John Rawls's *Political Liberalism*," *The Journal of Philosophy*, Vol. XCII, No. 3, March 1995.

Hanser, Matthew. "Why Are Killing and Letting Die Wrong?," *Philosophy & Public Affairs*, Vol. 24, No. 3, Summer 1995.

Harris, C.E., Jr., *Applying Moral Theories* (Belmont, CA: Wadsworth, 1986).

Henderson, Joseph. *The Use of Interactive Video in an Ethics Class with First-Year Medical Students.* Videotape (Hanover, NH: Interactive Media Lab, Dartmouth Medical School, 1991).

Johnson, Mark. *Moral Imagination: Implications of Cognitive Science for Ethics* (Chicago: University of Chicago Press, 1993).

Jonsen, Albert. "Of Balloons and Bicycles – Or – The Relationship between Ethical Theory and Practical Judgment," *Hastings Center Report*, September/October 1991.

Jonsen, Albert and Stephen Toulmin. *The Abuse of Casuistry: A History of Moral Reasoning* (University of California Press, 1988).

Kittay, Eva Feder and Diana T. Meyers (eds.). *Women and Moral Theory* (Savage MD: Rowman & Littlefield, 1987).

Kliever, Lonnie D. (ed.). *Dax's Case: Essays in Medical Ethics and Human Meaning* (Dallas, TX: Southern Methodist University Press, 1989).

Kurtines, William M. and Gewirtz, Jacob L. (eds.). *Morality, Moral Behavior, and Moral Development* (New York: John Wiley & Sons, 1984).

—— *Moral Development through Social Interaction* (New York: John Wiley & Sons, 1987).

Lauritzen, Paul. "Ethics and Experience: The Case of the Curious Response," *Hastings Center Report*, January/February 1996.

Lukas, J. Anthony. *Common Ground: A Turbulent Decade in the Lives of Three American Families* (New York: Alfred A. Knopf, 1985).

May, William F. *The Patient's Ordeal* (Bloomington: Indiana University Press, 1991.

Meisel, Alan. *The Right to Die*, Volumes I and II, Second Edition (New York: John Wiley & Sons, 1995).

Merleau-Ponty, Maurice. *The Primacy of Perception* (Chicago: Northwestern University Press, 1964).

Midgley, Mary. *Heart & Mind: The Varieties of Moral Experience* (New York: St. Martin's Press, 1981).

Morreim, E. Haavi. "Profoundly Diminished Life: The Casualties of Coercion," *Hastings Center Report*, January/February 1994.

Morrill, Richard. *Teaching Values in College* (San Francisco: Jossey-Bass, 1981).

Noddings, Nel. *Caring: A Feminine Approach to Ethics & Moral Education* (Berkeley: University of California Press, 1984).

Nussbaum, Martha. "Compassion: The Basic Social Emotion," *Social Philosophy & Policy*, Winter 1996.

—— *Love's Knowledge* (New York: Oxford University Press, 1990).

Pauchant, Thierry C. and Ian I. Mitroff. *Transforming the Crisis-Prone Organization: Preventing Individual, Organizational, and Environmental Tragedies* (San Francisco: Jossey-Bass, 1992).

Petraglia, Joseph. *Exploring the Effects of Realism on Arousal and Rhetorical Representation* (Pittsburgh, PA: Carnegie Mellon University, unpublished dissertation, 1991).

Putnam, Hilary. "How Not To Solve Ethical Problems," in *Reason With a Human Face* (Boston: Harvard University Press, 1990).

—— "A Reconsideration of Deweyan Democracy," in *Renewing Philosophy* (Boston: Harvard University Press, 1992).

Rawls, John. *Political Liberalism* (New York: Columbia University Press, 1993).

—— "Reply to Habermas," *The Journal of Philosophy*, Vol. XCII, No. 3, March 1995.

Regan, Tom (ed.). *Matters of Life and Death* (Philadelphia: Temple University Press, 1980).

Rorty, Richard. *Contingency, Irony, and Solidarity* (Cambridge: Cambridge University Press, 1989).

Rosenberg, Vivian. "Affective Awareness as a Critical Thinking Skill," *Teaching Thinking & Problem Solving*, January/February 1986.

Schoeman, Ferdinand (ed.). *Responsibility, Character, and the Emotions: New Essays in Moral Psychology* (Cambridge: Cambridge University Press, 1987).

Schon, Donald A. *The Reflective Practitioner: How Professionals Think in Action* (New York: Basic Books, 1983).

Simon, Herbert. *Models of Discovery* (Dordrecht: D. Reidel, 1977).

Solomon, Robert. *A Passion for Justice: Emotions and the Origins of the Social Contract* (New York: Addison-Wesley, 1990).

Steele, William. "Lives in the Balance," *Cornell Alumni News*, February 1983.

Tavris, Carol, with Richard Paul. *Critical Thinking and the Human Emotions*. Videotape (Rohnert Park, CA: Center for Critical Thinking and Moral Critique, Sonoma State University, 1990).

Troup, Stanley B. "Dax's Case," *Journal of the American Medical Association*, Vol. 262, No. 18, November 10, 1989.

Twiss, Sumner B. "Alternative Approaches to Patient and Family Medical Ethics: Review and Assessment," *Religious Studies Review*, Vol. 21, No. 4, October 1995.

White, Robert B. *Please Let Me Die!* Videotape (Galveston, TX: University of Texas Medical Branch, 1974).

White, Robert B. and H. Tristram Englehardt, Jr., "A Demand to Die," *Hastings Center Report*, June 1975.

Young, Richard, "Toward an Adequate Pedagogy for Rhetorical Argumentation: A Case Study in Invention," presented at the Third Annual Conference on Argumentation, University of Amsterdam, June 1994.